The Inner Game of Marketing

Mastering the Mind Behind the Message

The Inner Game of Marketing

Mastering the Mind Behind the Message

Subba Rao Chaganti

TM

PharmaMed Press

An imprint of BSP Books Pvt. Ltd.

4-4-309/316, Giriraj Lane,

Sultan Bazar, Hyderabad - 500 001,

Telangana, India.

The Inner Game of Marketing: Mastering the Mind Behind the Message
by Subba Rao Chaganti

Disclaimer: The authors and the publishers have taken due care to provide the authentic, reliable and up to date information related to the subject. However, neither the authors nor the publisher shall be responsible for any liability for any damage caused as a result of use of this book. The respective user must check the accuracy from other sources too.

Published by

™ **PharmaMed Press**

An imprint of BSP Books Pvt. Ltd.
4-4-309/316, Giriraj Lane, Sultan Bazar,
Hyderabad - 500 001, Telangana, India.
Phone: 040-23445688
E-mail: info@pharmamedpress.net
www.bspbooks.net/www.pharmamedpress.net

ISBN: 978-93-47311-17-8 (Paperback)

Disclaimer

This book is intended for educational, analytical, and informational purposes only. The views and interpretations expressed herein are solely those of the author and are presented in good faith, based on publicly available information, academic research, and professional experience.

Use of Brand Names and Case Examples

This book references trademarks, brand names, companies, and products for purposes of commentary, analysis, criticism, and education. All trademarks and brand names are the property of their respective owners. Any mention of organizations, brands, or products does not imply endorsement, sponsorship, affiliation, or approval by the respective rights holders.

All brand-related examples and case discussions are based on publicly available information and are used illustratively to explain concepts related to marketing, psychology, and decision-making. Interpretations and conclusions presented reflect the author's analytical perspective and should not be construed as official positions of the organizations discussed.

Academic Research and Intellectual Attribution

This book draws on established theories and findings from fields including, but not limited to, marketing, behavioral economics, cognitive psychology, neuroscience, and performance science. These theories, concepts, and research findings are paraphrased, synthesized, and interpreted in original language. Proper attribution has been provided through citations and notes where appropriate.

The book does not reproduce proprietary research, confidential data, or unpublished academic material. Any short quotations used fall within accepted norms of fair use for scholarly and critical commentary.

No Professional Advice

Nothing in this book should be construed as legal, financial, medical, or professional advice. Readers are encouraged to consult qualified professionals before making decisions that may affect their business, career, or personal circumstances. The author and publisher disclaim any liability arising from the application of ideas or strategies discussed in this book.

Limitation of Liability

While reasonable efforts have been made to ensure the accuracy of information presented, the author makes no representations or warranties, express or implied, regarding completeness, accuracy, or applicability to specific situations. The author and publisher shall not be liable for any direct, indirect, incidental, or consequential damages arising from the use of this material.

Ethical Use of Psychological and Neuroscientific Concepts

This book discusses psychological and neuroscientific principles to enhance understanding of how marketing communication is perceived and processed. These discussions are intended to promote ethical, responsible, and transparent application of such principles. The author does not advocate manipulation, exploitation, or misuse of psychological or neurological insights.

AI Use and Transparency

Portions of this work may have been developed with the assistance of AI-based tools for purposes such as editing, language refinement, ideation support, or synthesis. All intellectual content, structure, arguments, and conclusions are the author's own. No copyrighted material was knowingly reproduced or derived from proprietary sources through the use of AI.

Errors and Omissions

Despite best efforts, errors or omissions may occur. The author welcomes corrections and clarifications for future editions.

Acknowledgements

Writing a book that integrates insights from psychology, neuroscience, business strategy, and consciousness studies into practical marketing wisdom requires not just individual effort but also a community of supporters who believe in both the vision and the person pursuing it. I am deeply grateful to everyone who has contributed to making *The Inner Game of Marketing* possible.

Publishing Partnership

My profound gratitude begins with **Anil Shah**, my publisher, whose immediate understanding of this book's potential and unwavering commitment to its success made this project possible. From our first conversation about integrating consciousness principles with marketing practice, Anil has not just been a business partner but a true collaborator who shares the vision of elevating how marketing serves human flourishing. His guidance through the complex publishing process and faith in unconventional approaches to business literature have been invaluable.

Special thanks to **Nikunjesh Shah**, publisher, for his dedication to making the digital editions of this book widely accessible. In an age where ideas must reach global audiences to create meaningful impact, Nikunjesh's expertise in digital publishing ensures that these concepts can serve marketing professionals wherever they are in their journey toward greater consciousness and effectiveness.

Design and Production

To **Naresh Daver and his exceptional team at PharmaMedPress**: your commitment to creating a book that reflects the quality and consciousness of its content has been extraordinary. The design process itself embodied the collaboration and attention to excellence that this book advocates. Naresh's understanding that book design is not just about aesthetics but about supporting the reader's learning journey has resulted in a work that honors both the content and the reader's experience.

Intellectual Foundation

While this book represents years of personal exploration and practical application, it stands on the shoulders of countless researchers, thinkers, and practitioners whose work has illuminated the intersection of consciousness and effective communication. Tim Gallwey's original insights into the inner game provided the foundational framework. Daniel Kahneman's revelations about dual-system thinking, Mihaly Csikszentmihalyi's research on flow states, and the pioneering work of neuroscientists studying mirror neurons and social cognition have provided essential building blocks.

The marketing professionals, business leaders, and entrepreneurs who have shared their challenges, insights, and feedback over the years have been my greatest teachers. Their willingness to experiment with consciousness-based approaches to business challenges has provided real-world validation that these concepts not only work but also transform both outcomes and experiences.

Family Foundation

Above all, this work would not have been possible without the loving support and patient understanding of my family, who have created the foundation of stability and encouragement that enables creative and intellectual risk-taking.

To my wife, **Mahalakshmi**, whose unwavering belief in both this project and in me has sustained this work through every challenge and breakthrough. Her wisdom, patience, and practical support have been the bedrock that made years of research, writing, and refinement possible. More than tolerating the long hours and consuming focus that book writing requires, she has actively encouraged the pursuit of work that aligns with our shared values of service and authentic contribution.

To my children and their spouses—**Srinivasa Phanindra**, **Geetha**, **Lavanya**, **Satya Sankara Aditya**, **Sowmya**, and **Chaitanya**—who have supported this endeavor with enthusiasm and understanding. Their own professional journeys and life choices have been constant reminders that meaningful work and authentic success are not just possible but essential. Their diverse perspectives and experiences have enriched my understanding of how consciousness principles apply across different fields and generations.

To my grandchildren—**Aditi**, **Eesha**, **Surya**, and **Shriya**—who represent the future for whom this work is ultimately intended. Their natural curiosity, authentic expression, and unconscious wisdom have been constant reminders of the consciousness qualities that this book seeks to cultivate in professional practice. They embody the possibility of living and working from authenticity rather than merely performing it.

Professional Community

Gratitude extends to the marketing professionals, business leaders, and consciousness practitioners who have engaged with these ideas in workshops, consultations, and conversations. Their willingness to experiment with integrating inner development with outer effectiveness has provided invaluable feedback and real-world testing of every concept in this book.

The colleagues and mentors who have challenged my thinking, offered alternative perspectives, and supported the evolution of these ideas deserve special recognition. This work has been strengthened by every person who cared enough to offer honest feedback, thoughtful criticism, or encouraging support.

The Larger Community

Finally, acknowledgment to the broader community of researchers, practitioners, and leaders who are pioneering the integration of consciousness development with professional excellence across all fields. This book represents one small contribution to a larger movement toward work that serves both individual fulfillment and collective flourishing.

To the marketers who will apply these insights with integrity and wisdom: you are the ultimate collaborators in this work. Your commitment to practicing marketing as conscious service rather than sophisticated manipulation will determine whether these ideas contribute to the evolution of how business serves human needs.

A Living Thank You

These acknowledgments represent gratitude not just for past support but for the ongoing relationship and shared commitment to conscious business practice. The inner game of marketing, like any practice worth pursuing, is developed in community rather than isolation. Every person mentioned here has contributed not just to this book but to the development of consciousness that makes both meaningful work and authentic service possible.

The work continues through each person who chooses to approach marketing—and business generally—as an opportunity for consciousness development and genuine contribution to human flourishing. In this sense, these acknowledgements are just the beginning of a conversation that extends far beyond any individual book or author.

With deep gratitude and excitement for the continued journey ahead.

Subba Rao Chaganti

November 2025, Farmington

Preface

In 1974, Tim Gallwey published a slim volume called *The Inner Game of Tennis*, which revolutionized not only how athletes approached their sport but also how anyone seeking mastery in complex skills understood the relationship between internal consciousness and external performance. Gallwey's central insight was profoundly simple yet transformative: the primary obstacles to peak performance aren't external—they're internal. The quality of your tennis game, he discovered, depends less on perfecting your technique than on removing the psychological interference that prevents your natural abilities from expressing themselves.

This book applies Gallwey's revolutionary framework to marketing, but with a crucial evolution. Where Gallwey focused primarily on individual performance, we explore how the inner game principles apply to the fundamentally relational activity of marketing—how your internal consciousness affects not just your own performance, but your ability to create authentic connection and genuine influence with other human beings.

The inspiration for this work emerged from a persistent question that has puzzled me throughout two decades of marketing practice and study: Why do some campaigns feel effortless to create and natural to experience while others—often technically superior—feel forced and manipulative despite sophisticated execution? Why do certain marketers consistently produce work that audiences actively seek out and share, while others struggle to capture attention despite mastering every contemporary technique and framework?

The answer, I've discovered, lies in understanding marketing as fundamentally a consciousness discipline rather than just a technical one. The most effective marketing doesn't emerge from superior technique alone—it emerges from the integration of technical competence with psychological understanding, authentic self-expression, and genuine commitment to serving human needs.

The Convergence of Three Streams

This book represents the convergence of three distinct but related streams of inquiry that have occupied my professional and personal development for the past fifteen years.

The first stream is the practical demand for marketing that actually works in an environment of unprecedented complexity and skepticism. Traditional approaches to persuasion and influence are becoming less effective as audiences develop sophisticated resistance to obvious manipulation while simultaneously craving authentic connection and genuine value. The marketers who succeed in this environment are those who learn to influence through understanding rather than manipulation, who create engagement through service rather than extraction.

The second stream is the explosion of research in neuroscience, cognitive psychology, and behavioral economics that reveals how human minds actually process information, form preferences, and make decisions. This research demonstrates that effective marketing must align with rather than fight against neurological realities—that the brain's systems for attention, memory, emotion, and social connection operate according to principles that most marketing education never addresses.

The third stream is the growing recognition that business success and personal fulfillment need not be competing values—that the most sustainable competitive advantages emerge from work that serves both commercial objectives and authentic human development. The professionals who thrive long-term are those who find ways to express their genuine values and capabilities through work that contributes to rather than detracts from collective well-being.

The integration of these three streams creates what I call "conscious marketing"—an approach that achieves commercial effectiveness through authentic service to human needs rather than despite it.

Who this Book is For

The Inner Game of Marketing is written for marketing professionals who sense that there must be more to excellent marketing than the accumulation of techniques and tactics, who want to develop the kind of sustainable competitive advantage that emerges from authentic mastery rather than just superior execution of conventional approaches.

It's for those who have achieved competence in traditional marketing methods but find themselves asking deeper questions: How do I create work that feels authentic while remaining strategically effective? How do I build genuine audience relationships in an environment saturated with manipulation? How do I develop the kind of marketing intuition that enables breakthrough insights and innovative approaches?

It's also for business leaders and entrepreneurs who recognize that marketing represents far more than promotional activity—that it's the primary interface between their organization's authentic value and the people who might benefit from that value. These leaders understand that marketing excellence requires not just skilled execution but conscious intention, not just technical competence but psychological wisdom.

Finally, it's for anyone interested in the intersection of consciousness development and professional excellence—those who suspect that the highest levels of performance in any domain require integration of technical skill with authentic self-expression and genuine service to others.

What this Book is Not

Before describing what this book offers, it's important to clarify what it doesn't provide. This is not a collection of marketing tactics, growth hacks, or step-by-step formulas for campaign creation. While it includes practical applications and specific techniques, these emerge from psychological principles rather than standing as independent tools.

This is not a purely theoretical exploration of marketing psychology. While it draws extensively on research from neuroscience, cognitive psychology, and consciousness studies, every insight is grounded in practical application and tested through real market experience.

This is not a critique of analytical thinking or strategic planning. Rather, it's an exploration of how analytical rigor can integrate with rather than compete with intuitive insight, how strategic frameworks can support rather than constrain authentic expression.

Most importantly, this is not about becoming more sophisticated at psychological manipulation. The entire approach is grounded in the premise that the most effective long-term marketing serves rather than exploits human psychology, that sustainable competitive advantage emerges from authentic value creation rather than sophisticated persuasion techniques.

The Structure of the Journey

The book is organized into five parts that guide you through a systematic exploration of marketing consciousness, from internal psychology to practical application and lifelong mastery.

Part I: The Inner Arena of Marketing explores the internal psychological dynamics that govern your creative and strategic thinking. You'll discover how your own cognitive architecture either supports or sabotages your marketing effectiveness. You'll also learn to integrate analytical thinking with creative intuition while removing the internal interference that prevents your best work from emerging.

Part II: Neuroscience of Influence examines how human brains actually process and respond to marketing messages. Through exploration of storytelling psychology, dopamine systems, and memory formation, you'll understand how to create communication that works with rather than against neurological realities.

Part III: The Psychology of Winning Campaigns analyzes how psychological insights translate into campaigns that capture attention, build authentic relationships, and create lasting influence. You'll explore attention architecture, authenticity-performance integration, and the transmission of genuine conviction.

Part IV: Mastery through Practice addresses the challenge of translating understanding into consistent excellence. You'll learn to orchestrate your internal dialogue productively, develop sophisticated market listening capabilities, and build the resilience and adaptability required for sustained success.

Part V: The Winning Mindset explores the consciousness characteristics that enable the highest levels of marketing performance. You'll discover how to access flow states consistently, transcend competitive thinking toward collaborative value creation, and integrate marketing practice with lifelong learning and authentic self-expression.

A Personal Note

Writing this book has been simultaneously the most challenging and most rewarding professional project I've undertaken. It was challenging because it required integrating insights from disciplines I had never formally studied—neuroscience, consciousness research, spiritual psychology—with practical marketing experience gained through successes and failures across multiple industries. The integration is rewarding because it has transformed not just how I approach marketing work, but also how I understand the relationship between professional excellence and personal development.

The ideas in this book have been tested through workshops with marketing professionals at every career stage, and through conversations with colleagues who have pushed my thinking in directions I couldn't have reached alone.

Every insight has been earned through application rather than just study, refined through feedback rather than just theory, and validated through results that serve both commercial objectives and authentic human needs.

An Invitation to Practice

This book is best understood not as information to be consumed but as an invitation to practice—a framework for developing the kind of marketing consciousness that enables both professional excellence and personal fulfillment. The concepts will become valuable only to the extent that you apply them in real marketing contexts while paying attention to both internal experience and external results.

The inner game of marketing isn't something you master once and then possess forever. It's a lifelong practice of consciousness development that happens to express itself through marketing excellence. The journey has no final destination—only the continuous deepening of understanding, authenticity, and service that makes each day's work both an expression of who you are and a contribution to who you are becoming.

My hope is that this book will serve not just your marketing effectiveness but your professional fulfillment, not just your business success but your authentic contribution to the collective evolution of how marketing is practiced and how commercial activity serves human flourishing.

The inner game begins now. Welcome to the practice.

Subba Rao Chaganti
Farmington, November 2025

Contents

PART I: THE INNER ARENA OF MARKETING

Part I

The Inner Arena of Marketing

Every marketing campaign starts not in a boardroom or on a whiteboard, but in the mind of the marketer. Before the first word is written, the first audience segment is defined, or the first metric is tracked, there is an internal world of thoughts, assumptions, fears, and aspirations that will ultimately influence every strategic decision that comes afterward.

This inner landscape—what we call the "inner arena of marketing"—operates based on principles that most business schools do not teach and that many marketing frameworks overlook. Yet it is here, in this space between conscious intention and unconscious action, that the outcome of breakthrough campaigns versus forgettable ones is determined.

Think about the last time you saw truly memorable marketing. Maybe it was a brand story that brought you to tears, an ad that made you burst out laughing, or a product launch that had you hitting refresh at midnight. The power of these moments wasn't just clever placements or advanced targeting—it was the genuine human authenticity behind them, still driven by commercial purpose.

This authenticity cannot be created through focus groups or A/B tests, although both have value. It stems from something much more fundamental: the marketer's ability to access and trust their own deeper intuition while also understanding the psychological factors that influence human behavior.

The Paradox of Modern Marketing

We live in a groundbreaking era of marketing sophistication. We can track user behavior across devices, accurately predict customer lifetime value with algorithms, and customize messages on a large scale. We have access to neuroscientific research that reveals exactly how the brain responds to various stimuli, as well as psychological studies that provide a detailed examination of the decision-making process.

Yet, despite all this knowledge and ability, most marketing still struggles to build genuine connections. Consumers report feeling overwhelmed by advertising, doubting brand promises, and becoming more resistant to traditional persuasion strategies. The sophistication of our tools has created distance from the human truth at the core of all effective communication.

This paradox suggests that something fundamental is missing from our approach—not just more data or improved technology, but a deeper understanding of the internal dynamics that influence how marketers think, feel, and create.

The Two Games we're Really Playing

In any marketing effort, there are actually two games being played simultaneously. The first is the external game: reaching the right audience with the right message at the right moment through the right channels. This is the game of tactics, metrics, budgets, and competitive positioning—the visible arena where most marketing education and practice concentrate.

The second is the internal game: the conversation occurring inside the marketer's mind as they navigate uncertainty, creative blocks, performance anxiety, and the ongoing tension between authenticity and optimization. This internal game involves fears that make us play it safe, assumptions that limit our strategic vision, and unconscious patterns that either improve or undermine our creative output.

Most marketing failures stem not from external issues—such as poor targeting, limited budgets, or competitive shortcomings—but from internal problems. When marketers are anxious, they produce anxious campaigns. When they lose connection to their core values, their messages lack conviction. When they focus too much on metrics at the cost of true meaning, they risk becoming irrelevant.

Beyond the Myth of Pure Rationality

Traditional marketing education perpetuates a myth that has become increasingly counterproductive: the belief that effective marketing is purely a rational discipline, governed by logical frameworks and measurable outcomes. While analytical thinking certainly has its place, this rational-only approach ignores decades of research in cognitive science, behavioral economics, and neuroscience that reveal decision-making—both for marketers and consumers—to be far more intuitive and emotionally driven than we typically acknowledge.

The most successful marketers throughout history have been those who learned to dance between these two modes of thinking: leveraging analytical insights while remaining open to intuitive leaps, optimizing for performance while preserving emotional resonance, following data while trusting their deeper sense of what truly matters to their audience.

This integration requires what we might call "marketing wisdom"—the ability to hold both technical competence and human insight, to be strategic without losing spontaneity, to be results-focused without forgetting that results ultimately flow from genuine value creation.

The Promise of Inner Game Mastery

Part I of this book introduces you to the foundational concepts that govern the inner arena of marketing. You'll discover how your own cognitive architecture—the same dual-system thinking that governs all human decision-making—either supports or sabotages your marketing effectiveness. You'll learn to recognize and quiet the internal critic that generates fear-based campaigns, and you'll begin to access and trust the unconscious intelligence that produces breakthrough insights and authentic resonance.

This isn't about becoming a different kind of marketer—it's about becoming more fully the marketer you already are, freed from the internal interference that prevents your best work from emerging.

The stakes of this inner game are higher than they might initially appear. In a world where consumers are increasingly skilled at detecting and dismissing inauthentic communication, the brands and marketers who will thrive are those who can consistently create work that feels both strategically sound and genuinely human.

This requires not just better tools or clearer frameworks, but a fundamental shift in how we understand the creative process of marketing itself. It requires recognizing that our greatest competitive advantage lies not in our ability to manipulate consumer behavior, but in our capacity to understand and authentically serve human needs.

Welcome to the inner arena of marketing, where the most important victories are won not against competitors, but against the limitations we place on our own potential for creative and commercial impact.

Chapter 1

The Two Minds of Marketing

System 1 and System 2 thinking for marketers—the conscious strategist vs subconscious storyteller

Picture this scenario: You're sitting in a strategy meeting, armed with comprehensive market research, detailed customer personas, and a carefully constructed competitive analysis. The data clearly suggests that your next campaign should emphasize product features, target a specific demographic segment, and deploy across predetermined channels with measurable objectives. This is your analytical mind at work—systematic, logical, and reassuringly quantifiable.

But as you begin sketching the campaign, something else emerges. Perhaps it's an unexpected metaphor, an emotional angle the data didn't predict, or an intuitive sense that the "obvious" approach feels somehow hollow. This second voice doesn't speak in spreadsheets or conversion rates—it communicates through hunches, stories, and a felt sense of what might truly resonate with another human being.

Welcome to the fundamental reality of marketing consciousness: you don't have one mind creating your campaigns, you have two.

The Architecture of Marketing Thinking

Nobel laureate Daniel Kahneman revolutionized our understanding of human cognition by identifying two distinct systems of thinking that operate simultaneously in every decision we make. For marketers, understanding these systems isn't just intellectually interesting—it's practically essential, because the quality of our campaigns depends entirely on how skillfully we navigate between them.

System 1 is fast, automatic, and intuitive. It operates below the threshold of conscious awareness, processing vast amounts of information instantaneously and generating immediate impressions, gut reactions, and creative insights.

When you instantly "know" that a headline feels wrong, when a brand positioning clicks into place without effort, or when you can sense exactly what emotional tone will work for a particular audience—that's System 1 in action.

System 2 is slow, deliberate, and analytical. It's the voice of conscious reasoning that evaluates options, weighs evidence, and constructs logical arguments. When you're calculating customer acquisition costs, analyzing A/B test results, or working through the steps of a marketing funnel—that's System 2 doing what it does best.

Most marketing education focuses almost exclusively on developing System 2 capabilities, including frameworks for strategic analysis, methods for measuring performance, and processes for optimizing campaigns. This makes sense because System 2 thinking is easier to teach, test, and replicate. But here's what the textbooks rarely mention: the most powerful marketing emerges not from either system alone, but from the dynamic interplay between them.

The Conscious Strategist: System 2 in Marketing

Your System 2 mind is the marketing professional you probably think of as your "real" marketing self. It's methodical, evidence-based, and comfortable with complexity. This is the mind that builds customer journey maps, designs attribution models, and creates detailed campaign timelines.

System 2 excels at:

- **Pattern recognition in data**: Spotting trends in customer behavior, identifying seasonal fluctuations, and understanding what the numbers are really telling you
- **Strategic planning**: Breaking down complex market dynamics into manageable components and creating systematic approaches to reach your objectives
- **Risk assessment**: Evaluating potential downsides, considering competitive responses, and making resource allocation decisions
- **Performance optimization**: Running controlled experiments, interpreting statistical significance, and making iterative improvements based on measurable results

The conscious strategist is invaluable, but it has inherent limitations. System 2 thinking is effortful and requires more time. It can only hold a limited amount of information in working memory at any given time. Most importantly for marketers, it struggles with the kinds of nuanced, emotionally complex judgments that determine whether a message truly connects with its intended audience.

The Subconscious Storyteller: System 1 in Marketing

Your System 1 mind operates like a master pattern-matching engine, instantly processing subtle cues about human behavior, emotional resonance, and social dynamics. This is the part of you that immediately senses when a brand voice feels authentic or forced, when a creative concept has breakthrough potential, or when a market positioning is compelling even if you can't yet articulate why.

System 1 excels at:

- **Emotional intelligence**: Reading between the lines of customer feedback, sensing the underlying motivations behind stated preferences, and intuiting what people actually want versus what they say they want
- **Creative synthesis**: Combining seemingly unrelated ideas into novel concepts, finding unexpected connections between brand values and customer needs, and generating original approaches to familiar challenges
- **Social calibration**: Understanding cultural contexts, recognizing tribal dynamics, and sensing how messages will land within specific communities
- **Authenticity detection**: Instantly recognizing when communication feels genuine versus manufactured, when brand actions align with stated values, and when there's congruence between internal culture and external messaging

The subconscious storyteller processes information that would overwhelm conscious analysis—micro-expressions in focus group videos, subtle shifts in language patterns across customer segments, the emotional undertones that make one message memorable and another forgettable.

The Inner Conflict: When the Two Minds Clash

Problems arise when these two systems work against each other rather than in harmony. Consider these common scenarios that every marketer has experienced:

Analysis Paralysis: Your System 2 mind becomes so focused on gathering more data, running additional tests, and perfecting the strategic framework that it freezes the creative process entirely. You have comprehensive buyer personas, but somehow lose sight of the actual humans you're trying to reach.

Gut Decision Regret: Your System 1 mind generates a powerful creative insight or strategic direction that feels absolutely right in the moment, but when subjected to System 2 analysis, it seems to crumble under logical scrutiny. You second-guess intuitive leaps that might have led to breakthrough work.

Creative-Analytics Tension: The data suggests one approach, while your creative instincts pull you toward something entirely different. Rather than finding a synthesis, you find yourself torn between being "data-driven" and "creative," as if these were mutually exclusive approaches.

Authenticity-Optimization Conflict: System 1 knows when messaging feels authentic and resonant, but System 2 knows what performs well in terms of click-through rates and conversion metrics. When these points are in different directions, many marketers default to whatever improves the metrics, often at the cost of genuine connection.

The Integration Advantage

The marketers who consistently create work that is both strategically sound and emotionally resonant have learned something crucial: these two systems aren't adversaries to be chosen between, but collaborators to be integrated.

Consider how the most memorable campaigns emerge. The initial spark often comes from System 1—an intuitive understanding of a cultural moment, an emotional insight about customer experience, or a creative connection that no analysis could have predicted. However, transforming that spark into effective marketing requires System 2 capabilities, including strategic thinking about audience segmentation, tactical planning for execution across channels, and systematic measurement of results.

Nike's "Just Do It" campaign exemplifies this integration. The core insight—that people's relationship with exercise is fundamentally psychological rather than product-focused—emerged from System 1 understanding of human motivation and self-perception. But the execution required sophisticated System 2 thinking: careful selection of athletes who embodied different aspects of the message, strategic media placement that reinforced the positioning, and measurement systems that tracked both brand perception and business impact.

Practical Integration: Learning to Dance between Systems

The goal isn't to think less analytically or to ignore your intuitive insights, but to develop what we might call "cognitive flexibility"—the ability to fluidly shift between different modes of thinking depending on the situation's requirements.

For strategic planning: Begin with System 2 analysis to understand the competitive landscape, market dynamics, and customer segments. But before finalizing your approach, engage System 1 by asking: "What does this strategy feel like from the customer's perspective? What story are we really telling? Does this approach honor both our business objectives and genuine human needs?"

For creative development: Allow System 1 to generate initial concepts without immediate analytical judgment. Give your subconscious storyteller space to make unexpected connections and propose unconventional approaches. Then bring System 2 online to evaluate feasibility, refine messaging for clarity, and develop systematic execution plans.

For performance evaluation: Use System 2 to track quantitative metrics and identify optimization opportunities. However, also engage System 1 to assess qualitative indicators—such as customer sentiment, brand resonance, and cultural relevance—that may not be immediately apparent in conversion data but can predict long-term success.

The most profound shift happens when you stop seeing these as separate, competing capabilities and start recognizing them as different aspects of a unified marketing intelligence. Your analytical mind provides the scaffolding; your intuitive mind provides the spark. Your strategic thinking creates the framework; your storytelling instincts bring it to life.

Beyond the False Choice

The most liberating realization for marketers is that you don't have to choose between being analytical and creative, data-driven and human-centered, or systematic and intuitive. The false choice that has polarized much of marketing discourse—art versus science, brand versus performance, creative versus analytical—dissolves when you understand that these represent different modes of the same essential capability: understanding and serving human needs in commercially viable ways.

The two minds of marketing aren't problems to be solved but resources to be integrated. In the chapters that follow, we'll explore how to quiet the internal interference that prevents this integration and learn to trust the deeper intelligence that emerges when both systems work in harmony.

Your conscious strategist and subconscious storyteller are not in competition—they're collaborators waiting to be introduced.

Chapter 2

Quieting the Inner Critic

Overcoming fear of failure, rejection, or customer indifference—mindset blocks of marketers vs creators

The presentation is scheduled for tomorrow morning. Your campaign concept is solid—months of research support the strategy, the creative execution feels fresh, and early testing suggests strong potential. Yet as you rehearse your pitch, a familiar voice emerges: What if they hate it? What if the CEO asks a question you can't answer? What if this whole approach is completely wrong?

This voice isn't offering helpful strategic analysis or constructive feedback. It's not your System 2 mind working through legitimate concerns or your System 1 mind sensing genuine problems with the work. This is something else entirely—a commentary track of doubt, criticism, and catastrophic prediction that seems designed not to improve your marketing but to prevent it from ever seeing the light of day.

Every marketer knows this voice intimately. It's the inner critic, and it may be the single greatest obstacle between you and your most impactful work.

The Anatomy of Marketing Self-Doubt

The inner critic speaks in the language of protection, but its effect is paralysis. It masquerades as prudent risk management while actually amplifying perceived threats far beyond their actual probability or consequence. For marketers, this voice typically organizes itself around several core fears that strike at the heart of what makes marketing both vulnerable and powerful.

Fear of Creative Exposure: Unlike many business disciplines, where failure can be attributed to external factors—such as market conditions, competitive responses, or resource constraints—marketing failure often feels deeply personal. When a campaign doesn't resonate, it suggests that your understanding of human nature, your sense of what matters to people, and your ability to create connection were somehow deficient. The inner critic exploits this vulnerability: *Who are you to think you understand what people want? Your taste isn't their taste. Your humor isn't their humor.*

Fear of Professional Judgment: Marketing sits at the intersection of art and commerce, creativity and accountability, intuition and measurement. This positioning makes it particularly susceptible to criticism from multiple directions. The inner critic anticipates these attacks: *The finance team will say it's not measurable enough. The creative team will say it's too corporate. The executives will say it's too risky. The customers will say it's tone-deaf.*

Fear of Irrelevance: In a landscape where consumer attention is increasingly fragmented and skeptical, the fear of being ignored can be more paralyzing than the fear of being criticized. The inner critic whispers, 'No one will care.' *It will disappear into the noise. You're just adding to the pollution of messages people don't want.*

Fear of Inauthenticity: As consumers become more sophisticated at detecting manufactured emotions and strategic manipulation, the line between influence and manipulation becomes both more important and more ambiguous. The inner critic exploits this uncertainty: *You're just trying to get people to buy things they don't need. This feels calculated. Real artists don't worry about conversion rates.*

The Creative-Commercial Tension

This last fear points to a deeper source of inner critic activity that's particularly acute for marketers: the tension between creative authenticity and commercial effectiveness. Unlike pure artists who can create primarily for self-expression, or pure analysts who can focus primarily on optimization, marketers must constantly navigate the space between these domains.

The inner critic thrives in this ambiguous territory, suggesting that any compromise between artistic integrity and business results represents a fundamental betrayal of one or the other. It creates a false dichotomy: either you're a "real" creative who doesn't concern yourself with metrics, or you're a "sellout" who has sacrificed authenticity for performance.

This false dichotomy is particularly destructive because it prevents marketers from accessing their full creative and analytical capabilities. When you're worried about whether your work is "authentic enough" or "commercial enough," you're not fully present to the actual challenge at hand: creating communication that genuinely serves both customer needs and business objectives.

The Perfectionism Trap

The inner critic's most sophisticated strategy is to disguise paralysis as perfectionism. It suggests that you shouldn't launch the campaign, publish the content, or present the strategy because it's not quite ready yet. It requires further research, refinement, and testing. The inner critic makes this sound reasonable, even professional.

But perfectionism in marketing is often procrastination in disguise. The inner critic knows that there will always be more data to gather, more scenarios to test, more stakeholders to consult. By holding your work to impossible standards of certainty and polish, it can indefinitely delay the moment when your work must face the ultimate test: actual human response in real market conditions.

Consider the marketing manager who spends weeks perfecting an email subject line, running test after test to optimize open rates, only to discover that the more fundamental issue was the relevance of the email's content to its intended audience. The perfectionism surrounding tactical details became a way of avoiding the larger creative and strategic risks inherent in the work.

The Voice vs. The Critic

Learning to quiet the inner critic begins with distinguishing it from other internal voices that actually serve your marketing effectiveness. Your System 2 analytical mind can identify risks or areas for improvement. Your System 1 intuitive mind might sense that something about the approach isn't quite right. These are valuable inputs that can enhance your work.

The inner critic is different. It doesn't offer specific, actionable feedback—it offers generalized predictions of doom. It doesn't help you improve the work—it suggests that attempting the work at all is fundamentally misguided. It doesn't operate from expertise or insight—it operates from fear.

Legitimate concern sounds like: "This headline might confuse our audience because it uses jargon they're not familiar with."

Inner critic sounds like: "This headline is terrible and everyone will think you don't understand the audience at all."

Legitimate concern sounds like: "We should test this with a small segment before the full launch to validate our assumptions."

Inner critic sounds like: "This whole approach is probably wrong and will definitely fail, so why bother testing?"

The legitimate concerns point toward specific actions that can improve the work. The inner critic points toward abandoning the work entirely.

The Paradox of Creative Courage

Here's what makes quieting the inner critic particularly challenging for marketers: a certain degree of concern about audience reception is actually essential to effective marketing. Complete indifference to how your work will be received by customers, colleagues, or the market would make you a poor marketer indeed.

The challenge is learning to hold space for legitimate professional concern while not allowing fear to dominate the creative process. This requires what we might call "creative courage"—not the absence of fear, but the ability to act effectively in the presence of uncertainty.

Creative courage in marketing looks like:

- **Accepting uncertainty as inherent**: Recognizing that you cannot know with complete certainty how any campaign will perform, and that this uncertainty is a feature of marketing, not a bug
- **Distinguishing between preparation and procrastination**: Preparing thoroughly while recognizing when additional preparation becomes a way of avoiding action.
- **Embracing iteration over perfection**: Viewing campaigns as experiments that will be refined based on market feedback rather than final statements that must be flawless from the start.
- **Focusing on service over approval**: Orienting your work around serving genuine customer needs rather than avoiding criticism or seeking universal approval.

Practical Strategies for Critic Management

The goal isn't to eliminate the inner critic—that's neither possible nor advisable. The goal is to prevent it from hijacking your creative process while remaining open to legitimate feedback and genuine intuitive guidance.

The Pre-Mortem Practice: Before beginning any significant campaign, conduct a "pre-mortem" where you deliberately imagine various ways the work might fail and develop contingency plans. This satisfies the inner critic's need to consider risks while channeling that energy into constructive preparation rather than paralyzing worry.

The 70% Rule: Adopt a standard that work should be launched when it's 70% ready rather than 100% perfect. This creates permission to iterate based on market feedback rather than trying to anticipate every possible scenario in advance.

The Audience of One: When the inner critic amplifies fears about universal approval or rejection, focus on creating work that would genuinely serve one specific person from your target audience. This shifts attention from abstract judgment to concrete value creation.

The Failure Resume: Maintain a document that tracks marketing experiments that didn't work as expected, along with what you learned from each. This normalizes failure as information rather than a verdict, building confidence in your ability to learn and adapt.

The Creator's Statement: Before beginning any campaign, write a brief statement about what you're trying to achieve and why it matters—not to the business or the metrics, but to the people you're trying to serve. Return to this statement when the inner critic suggests that your work lacks purpose or authenticity.

From Self-Protection to Service

The most powerful antidote to inner critic activity is shifting your fundamental orientation from self-protection to service. When your primary concern is avoiding criticism, rejection, or failure, the inner critic has plenty of material to work with. When your primary concern is creating genuine value for your audience, the inner critic's commentary becomes less relevant and less compelling.

This shift doesn't eliminate the risks inherent in marketing—campaigns can still fail, audiences can still be indifferent, and colleagues can still be critical. However, it alters your perception of those risks. Instead of seeing them as threats to your identity or competence, you begin to see them as information about how well you're serving your intended purpose.

A campaign that doesn't perform as expected becomes a source of insight about audience needs rather than evidence of your inadequacy. Criticism from colleagues becomes feedback on how to refine the work, rather than a judgment about your abilities. Market indifference can become a signal to dig deeper into customer understanding, rather than proof that you don't understand customers at all.

The Liberation of Imperfect Action

Perhaps the most profound shift that comes from quieting the inner critic is the liberation that emerges from taking imperfect action. When you stop waiting for complete certainty, perfect execution, or universal approval, you discover something remarkable: the market itself becomes your teacher, your collaborator, and your guide.

Instead of trying to create work that anticipates every possible response, you create work that invites genuine response. Instead of trying to avoid all possibilities of failure, you create systems for learning rapidly from whatever happens. Instead of trying to control outcomes, you focus on controlling the quality of your attention, intention, and effort.

This doesn't mean becoming careless or abandoning professional standards. It means recognizing that in a domain as complex and dynamic as human behavior, the only way to create consistently effective work is through engaged experimentation rather than perfect prediction.

The inner critic will never be completely silent—and that's fine. But it doesn't have to be the dominant voice in your creative process. When you learn to distinguish its fearful commentary from legitimate professional judgment, when you develop systems for acting effectively despite uncertainty, and when you orient your work around service rather than self-protection, something remarkable happens: your best marketing finally has space to emerge.

In the next chapter, we'll explore how to access and trust the unconscious intelligence that produces breakthrough insights—the creative resource that the inner critic works so hard to suppress.

Chapter 3

Trusting the Unconscious Mind

Flow States in Marketing Creativity—Why Overthinking Kills Resonance

The breakthrough came at 2:47 AM on a Tuesday, three weeks into what had become the most challenging campaign brief of Sarah's career. She'd been wrestling with how to reposition a heritage brand for Gen Z without alienating loyal customers, had filled notebooks with strategic frameworks, and had run dozens of focus groups that yielded nothing but conflicting insights.

Then, in that liminal space between sleep and waking, it arrived fully formed: not just a tagline or a creative concept, but an entire approach that honored both the brand's history and its future, that spoke authentically to younger consumers while deepening rather than abandoning its core identity. In thirty seconds of unconscious processing, her mind had solved what weeks of deliberate analysis couldn't crack.

Most marketers have experienced moments like this—sudden insights that emerge seemingly from nowhere, creative solutions that arrive complete and compelling, strategic directions that feel immediately and obviously right even though they couldn't have been derived through logical analysis alone. Yet despite the undeniable power of these experiences, many marketers remain deeply uncomfortable trusting anything they can't fully explain or systematically reproduce.

This discomfort represents one of the greatest untapped resources in marketing: the vast intelligence of the unconscious mind.

The Iceberg of Marketing Intelligence

Contemporary cognitive science suggests that conscious awareness represents only a tiny fraction of total mental processing power—perhaps 5% or less. The remaining 95% operates below the threshold of conscious access, continuously processing sensory information, recognizing patterns, making connections, and generating insights at speeds and scales that would overwhelm deliberate thinking.

For marketers, this unconscious processing is particularly powerful because it operates on exactly the kinds of complex, nuanced, and emotionally laden information that determine whether marketing truly resonates. While your conscious mind might struggle to articulate why one brand voice feels authentic and another feels forced, your unconscious mind processes hundreds of subtle linguistic, cultural, and emotional cues instantaneously to generate that assessment.

Consider what happens when you encounter truly exceptional marketing. Your immediate response isn't analytical—you don't consciously evaluate the targeting strategy, assess the creative execution against established frameworks, or measure the message against your stated preferences. You simply know, often within seconds, that this communication has connected with something important. That recognition is your unconscious mind speaking.

The Pattern Recognition Engine

The unconscious mind excels at pattern recognition on a scale that conscious thinking cannot match. Where deliberate analysis might compare a few variables across a limited dataset, unconscious processing can simultaneously integrate patterns from your entire life experience: every advertisement you've seen, every brand interaction you've had, every cultural moment you've witnessed, every emotional response you've observed in yourself and others.

This pattern recognition operates through what neuroscientists call "thin-slice judgments"—rapid, automatic assessments based on minimal information that are often more accurate than extended deliberate analysis. Malcolm Gladwell popularized this concept in "Blink," but its implications for marketing extend beyond quick decision-making.

When experienced marketers can immediately sense that a creative concept has breakthrough potential, when they can predict audience response to messaging before any testing occurs, when they can identify emerging cultural trends before they show up in data—they're accessing pattern recognition capabilities that have been developed through years of unconscious learning and refined through countless exposures to what works and what doesn't.

The Problem with Overthinking

The phrase "overthinking kills resonance" might seem counterintuitive in a discipline that prizes strategic rigor and analytical depth. But there's a crucial distinction between thinking deeply about the right things and thinking compulsively about everything.

Overthinking in marketing typically manifests as:

Analysis Recursion: Continuing to analyze data, test variables, and refine frameworks long past the point where additional analysis yields meaningful insights. The unconscious mind has already processed the available information and generated conclusions, but the conscious mind continues to cycle through the same data, seeking greater certainty.

Creative Micromanagement: Attempting to consciously control every aspect of the creative process—word choice, visual elements, emotional tone—rather than allowing creative insights to emerge organically and then using conscious thinking to refine and execute them effectively.

Authenticity Auditing: Constantly questioning whether work feels "real" or "authentic" instead of trusting the immediate felt sense that something either resonates or doesn't. This kind of meta-analysis often destroys the very quality it's trying to evaluate.

Audience Simulation: Trying to predict customer response through deliberate role-playing or demographic analysis rather than trusting an intuitive understanding of human nature developed through genuine attention to customer experience.

The common thread in these patterns is the attempt to use conscious thinking for tasks that unconscious processing handles more effectively. It's like trying to control your heartbeat or manually direct your immune system consciously—the deliberate intervention actually interferes with naturally occurring intelligence.

Flow States in Marketing

Athletes and musicians have long understood that peak performance occurs in flow states—periods of effortless concentration where conscious self-monitoring recedes and performance becomes spontaneous, intuitive, and highly effective. Marketing creativity operates according to similar principles.

In marketing flow states:

Strategic insights emerge naturally rather than being forced through analytical frameworks. You find yourself understanding market dynamics, customer needs, or competitive positioning with a clarity that goes beyond what the data alone could provide.

Creative concepts arrive complete rather than being assembled piece by piece. Headlines, visual concepts, and campaign approaches present themselves as coherent wholes that feel immediately right rather than constructed possibilities that might work.

Execution becomes intuitive rather than effortful. You know how to adjust messaging for different audiences, how to adapt concepts across channels, and how to maintain brand consistency without consulting style guides or approval processes.

Decision-making accelerates without sacrificing quality. Questions that might normally require extensive deliberation—such as which direction to pursue, how to respond to feedback, or whether an approach is worth testing—resolve themselves naturally through clear, intuitive guidance.

Flow states in marketing aren't mystical experiences—they're practical manifestations of accessing the unconscious mind's superior pattern recognition and creative synthesis capabilities.

The Conditions for Unconscious Access

Unlike conscious thinking, which can be directed through willpower and discipline, unconscious intelligence operates according to different principles. You cannot force insights to emerge, but you can create conditions that make them more likely.

Preparation Without Attachment: Thoroughly research the challenge, understand the constraints, and immerse yourself in relevant information, but then release the need to solve the problem through deliberate analysis. The preparation provides raw material for unconscious processing; the release creates space for insights to emerge.

Attention Without Tension: Maintain focused awareness on the challenge without gripping it tightly. This is similar to the "soft focus" that athletes use—alert but relaxed, engaged but not effortful.

Patience Without Passivity: Trust that insights will emerge while remaining actively available to recognize and receive them. This isn't passive waiting but active listening—staying tuned to the subtle signals that indicate when understanding is crystallizing.

Movement Between Modes: Alternate between periods of focused analysis and periods of mental spaciousness. Some of the most powerful marketing insights emerge during activities that engage the body while allowing the mind to process unconsciously—such as walking, driving, showering, or exercising.

The Integration Challenge

The goal isn't to abandon analytical thinking in favor of pure intuition, but to develop what we might call "conscious-unconscious collaboration." This requires learning to recognize when each mode of thinking is most appropriate and developing the skill to move fluidly between them.

For a strategic foundation, use conscious analysis to understand the market context, competitive landscape, and customer segments. Develop comprehensive knowledge that serves as the foundation for unconscious processing.

For creative breakthrough: Create space for unconscious insights to emerge around strategic direction, creative concepts, and innovative approaches. Trust the pattern recognition that suggests certain directions have unusual potential.

For tactical execution: Return to conscious analysis to translate insights into systematic implementation plans, measurement frameworks, and optimization processes.

For performance evaluation, use both analytical metrics and intuitive assessments to understand what's working. Numbers tell you what happened; unconscious pattern recognition often reveals why it happened and what it means for future direction.

The Paradox of Trying

The most challenging aspect of trusting unconscious intelligence is that it operates through a paradox: the harder you try to access it, the more elusive it becomes. Insights tend to emerge when you're not straining to produce them, creativity flows when you're not forcing it, and breakthrough understanding often arrives when you've stopped actively seeking it.

This doesn't mean being passive or unfocused. It means developing what Zen practitioners call "effortless effort"—a state of engaged relaxation where you're fully present to the challenge without being attached to producing specific outcomes through conscious control.

For marketers, this might mean:

- Setting aside dedicated time for non-directive thinking about current challenges
- Trusting first impressions of creative concepts, strategic directions, or campaign approaches
- Paying attention to what emerges during conversations, presentations, or collaborative sessions without immediately evaluating or editing it
- Following curiosity even when it leads in directions that don't seem immediately relevant to the task at hand
- Noticing when the analysis starts feeling repetitive or circular and shifting to a different mode of engagement

Beyond the False Choice

Just as we saw with the two minds of marketing and the challenge of the inner critic, learning to trust unconscious intelligence requires moving beyond false choices that limit marketing effectiveness. You don't have to choose between being strategic and intuitive, between being rigorous and creative, between being professional and spontaneous.

The most consistently effective marketers are those who have learned to access and integrate multiple forms of intelligence: analytical rigor when systematic thinking is required, intuitive insight when pattern recognition is needed, emotional intelligence when human connection is the priority, and practical wisdom when implementation and execution demand attention.

The unconscious mind isn't a mystical force—it's a sophisticated information processing system that operates according to different principles than conscious analysis. Learning to trust it doesn't require abandoning intellectual rigor; it requires expanding your definition of intelligence to include capabilities that operate below the threshold of conscious awareness but above the level of mere chance or guesswork.

The Courage to Not Know

Perhaps the deepest challenge in trusting unconscious intelligence is developing comfort with not knowing—not being able to explain exactly why a particular approach feels right, not having complete rational justification for every creative choice, not being able to predict with certainty how the market will respond.

This kind of not-knowing isn't ignorance—it's recognition that marketing operates in a domain of complexity that exceeds what any conscious analysis can fully capture. Customer behavior, cultural dynamics, emotional resonance, and authentic communication all involve variables that are real and influential but difficult to quantify or predict systematically.

Trusting unconscious intelligence means developing confidence in your ability to navigate this complexity through forms of knowing that complement rather than compete with analytical thinking. It means recognizing that some of your best marketing insights will arrive as gifts from processes you don't control rather than products of efforts you can direct.

When you learn to receive these gifts—and to distinguish them from wishful thinking, fear-based impulses, or simple preferences—you gain access to a resource that can dramatically expand both the creativity and effectiveness of your marketing.

In Part II, we'll explore how this unconscious intelligence operates in your audience as well, examining the neuroscience of how human brains actually respond to marketing messages and why understanding these processes can revolutionize your approach to influence and persuasion.

PART II: NEUROSCIENCE OF INFLUENCE

Part II

Neuroscience of Influence

In Part I, we explored the internal landscape of marketing consciousness—how your own mind processes information, generates insights, and either supports or sabotages your creative work. We discovered that effective marketing emerges not from pure analytical thinking alone, but from integrating conscious strategy with unconscious intelligence, free from the interference of fear-based internal criticism.

Now we turn our attention outward, to the minds of the people your marketing hopes to reach. For if understanding your own cognitive architecture is essential to creating authentic and resonant work, understanding how human brains actually process and respond to marketing messages is essential to ensuring that work achieves its intended impact.

This shift from internal to external focus reveals a profound symmetry: the same dual-system thinking that governs your creative process also governs your audience's reception of that creativity. The same unconscious pattern recognition that generates your best strategic insights also determines whether customers feel immediately drawn to or subtly repelled by your brand. The same flow states that produce breakthrough campaigns also create the moments when consumers move from passive exposure to active engagement.

But this symmetry runs deeper than mere analogy. The emerging field of neuromarketing, which applies neuroscientific research to understanding consumer behavior, reveals that effective marketing works by creating neurological resonance between the marketer and the audience. When your message truly connects, it's not just metaphorically speaking to something in the customer's experience; it's literally activating neural networks associated with recognition, understanding, and motivation.

Beyond the Myth of Rational Choice

Traditional marketing education has been built on a foundation that neuroscience now reveals to be fundamentally incomplete: the assumption that consumers make purchasing decisions primarily through conscious, rational evaluation of options. This "rational actor" model suggests that customers systematically compare features, benefits, and prices before making deliberate choices based on logical criteria.

While conscious evaluation certainly plays a role in some purchasing decisions, decades of brain imaging research reveal a more complex and fascinating reality. The vast majority of consumer choice is driven by unconscious processes—emotional responses, social instincts, memory associations, and neurological patterns that operate far below the threshold of conscious awareness.

Consider your own recent purchasing behavior. How did you choose your last restaurant meal? Your current smartphone? The coffee you drank this morning? If you're honest, these decisions involve far more intuitive assessment than systematic analysis. You didn't create spreadsheets comparing nutritional content across menu options; you ordered what "sounded good." You didn't conduct comprehensive feature comparisons across all available smartphones; instead, you chose based on a combination of brand familiarity, aesthetic preference, social signaling, and a gut feeling about what would best serve your needs.

This doesn't make you irrational—it makes you human. The human brain has evolved sophisticated systems for making complex decisions rapidly based on incomplete information, and these systems are remarkably effective at serving our actual needs rather than our stated criteria.

The Neuroscience Revolution in Marketing

The past two decades have witnessed a surge in research into how the brain actually responds to marketing stimuli. Using technologies like functional magnetic resonance imaging (fMRI), electroencephalography (EEG), and eye-tracking systems, researchers can now observe in real-time what happens in the brain when people encounter advertisements, brand messages, product designs, and purchasing environments.

The findings have been both illuminating and humbling for marketers. Illuminating because they reveal the actual mechanisms through which marketing creates influence—the specific neural pathways activated by effective storytelling, the precise brain regions involved in brand loyalty, the measurable neurological differences between authentic and manipulative communication. Humbling because they demonstrate how much traditional marketing practice has been based on assumptions rather than an understanding of how human minds actually work.

Perhaps most significantly, neuroscientific research validates what the most intuitive marketers have always suspected: people don't buy products, they buy feelings. They don't choose brands, they choose identities. They don't respond to features and benefits; they respond to stories that help them make sense of their own experience and aspirations.

The Three Brains of the Consumer

To understand how marketing messages travel from perception to action, it's useful to recognize that consumers process your communication through what neuroscientist Paul MacLean termed the "triune brain"—three distinct but interconnected neurological systems that evolved at different periods and serve different functions.

The Reptilian Brain (brainstem and cerebellum) governs survival instincts, automatic responses, and basic drives. This ancient system responds to marketing that addresses fundamental needs: safety, status, reproduction, and resource acquisition. It processes information rapidly and triggers immediate approach or avoidance responses before conscious thought occurs.

The Limbic Brain (also known as the limbic system) is responsible for managing emotions, forming memories, and facilitating social bonding. This mammalian system responds to marketing that creates emotional resonance, activates positive memories, or strengthens social connections. It determines whether messages feel familiar or foreign, trustworthy or threatening, personally relevant or abstract.

The Neocortex (cerebral cortex) handles rational analysis, language processing, and future planning. This newest system responds to marketing that provides logical justification for decisions already made by the deeper brain systems, or that presents novel information requiring conscious evaluation.

Understanding this hierarchy is crucial for marketers because research consistently shows that emotional and instinctive responses precede and influence rational evaluation, not the other way around. Customers often feel before they think, and they then think to justify what they've already felt.

The Mirror Neuron Revolution

Perhaps the most profound discovery for marketing practitioners has been the identification of mirror neurons—brain cells that fire both when performing an action and when observing someone else perform the same action. These neurons create automatic neurological empathy, allowing people to feel what they observe others experiencing literally.

For marketers, mirror neurons explain why authentic storytelling is so much more powerful than abstract messaging. When customers watch someone using your product and genuinely enjoying the experience, their mirror neurons fire as if they were having that positive experience themselves. When they observe someone solving a problem with your service, they neurologically experience the satisfaction that comes with that solution.

But mirror neurons also explain why inauthentic marketing fails so consistently. When the emotions displayed in your marketing don't match the genuine experience of using your product, when the stories you tell don't reflect real customer experience, when your brand promises don't align with actual delivery, mirror neurons detect the incongruence and generate subtle but powerful feelings of distrust.

This creates both an opportunity and a responsibility for marketers. The opportunity lies in neurologically transmitting authentic, positive experiences through marketing in ways that create genuine anticipation and desire. The responsibility is that any disconnection between your marketing and your actual offering will be detected at a neurological level, even when customers can't consciously articulate why something feels “off."

The Attention Economy and the Distracted Brain

Modern marketing operates in an environment that human brains are not evolutionarily equipped to handle: constant exposure to more information than can be processed consciously. The average person encounters thousands of marketing messages daily, yet can consciously attend to only a tiny fraction of them.

Neuroscience reveals that in this environment of information overload, the brain employs sophisticated filtering mechanisms to determine what deserves conscious attention. These filters operate largely outside conscious awareness and are influenced by factors that traditional marketing rarely considers: neural novelty detection, emotional relevance assessment, social significance evaluation, and personal identity alignment.

Understanding these filtering mechanisms is essential for modern marketers, as traditional approaches to gaining attention—such as repetition, volume, and interruption—often trigger the brain's filtering systems in ways that create resistance rather than engagement. The messages that successfully penetrate these filters are those that align with how the brain naturally processes and prioritizes information.

From Manipulation to Resonance

Perhaps the most important insight emerging from neuroscientific research is the distinction between marketing that exploits neurological vulnerabilities and marketing that resonates with genuine neurological realities.

Manipulative marketing attempts to trigger unconscious responses that serve the marketer's agenda rather than the customer's needs. It exploits fear, creates artificial scarcity, or activates social pressure to generate behavior that customers might not choose if they had complete information and unlimited time for consideration.

Resonant marketing, by contrast, aligns with the brain's natural information processing and decision-making systems. It provides genuine value, fosters authentic emotional connections, and enables customers to make choices that truly serve their needs and aspirations. It works with neurological realities rather than against them.

The distinction matters not just ethically but practically. As consumers become more sophisticated and markets become more transparent, manipulative tactics become less effective and more likely to create long-term brand damage. Resonant marketing, grounded in a genuine understanding of how human minds actually work, creates a sustainable competitive advantage by building authentic relationships rather than exploiting psychological vulnerabilities.

The Promise of Neurologically-Informed Marketing

Part II will examine how these neuroscientific insights are applied in practical marketing contexts. You'll discover how the brain processes stories and why narrative structure activates specific neural networks that create lasting memory and emotional connection. You'll learn how dopamine pathways create anticipation and desire, and how to design customer experiences that work in harmony with, rather than against, these neurological realities.

You'll understand why certain messages feel immediately compelling while others seem to bounce off consumer consciousness, and how to craft communication that naturally aligns with the brain's attention and memory systems. Most importantly, you'll learn to distinguish between marketing approaches that exploit neurological mechanisms and those that honor them—creating influence through understanding rather than manipulation.

This isn't about becoming a more sophisticated persuader in the traditional sense. It's about becoming a more effective communicator by understanding how communication actually works at the neurological level. When you align your marketing with how human brains naturally process information, form preferences, and make decisions, you don't have to work harder to create influence—you have to work smarter.

The goal isn't to manipulate consumer neurology but to speak its language fluently, creating marketing that feels as natural and compelling to your audience as it does authentic and purposeful to you. When marketing achieves this alignment—between your creative intentions and your audience's neurological realities—something remarkable happens: influence becomes a natural byproduct of genuine service rather than a goal to be achieved through strategic effort.

Welcome to the neuroscience of influence, where understanding how the mind works transforms not just how effectively you can market, but also how authentically you can connect.

Chapter 4

The Brain on Stories

Mirror neurons and the empathy effect—why emotional narratives outperform rational arguments

When neuroscientist Paul Zak placed participants in fMRI scanners and showed them a simple two-minute video about a father and his terminally ill son, something remarkable happened. As the story unfolded—the father's struggle to remain strong, his son's innocent joy despite his condition, the precious time they shared—the participants' brains began producing measurable amounts of oxytocin, the neurochemical associated with empathy, trust, and social bonding.

But that wasn't the most surprising part. When these same participants were later allowed to donate money to a charity for sick children, those who had produced the most oxytocin during the story donated the most money. The narrative hadn't just entertained them or informed them—it had literally changed their neurochemistry in ways that translated into behavior.

This experiment reveals something profound about the relationship between storytelling and influence: stories don't just convey information, they create embodied experiences. When we encounter a well-crafted narrative, our brains don't simply process it as external data—they simulate the experience internally, activating the same neural networks involved in actually living through similar events.

For marketers, this finding represents both a tremendous opportunity and a significant responsibility. It suggests that authentic storytelling may be the most powerful form of influence available, while simultaneously revealing why inauthentic narratives feel so immediately repelling.

The Neurological Reality of Narrative

To understand why stories wield such unique power in marketing, we need to examine what actually happens in the brain when people encounter narrative content. The findings from neuroscientific research are both fascinating and practical for anyone seeking to create genuinely compelling communication.

When you read or hear a story, multiple brain regions activate simultaneously in ways that don't occur with other forms of communication. The auditory cortex processes spoken words, but when those words describe sounds—"the coffee grinder whirred to life"—the auditory cortex activates as if you were actually hearing that sound. The visual cortex engages when stories include visual descriptions, motor regions fire when narratives involve physical actions, and emotional centers respond to the feelings experienced by story characters.

This neurological mirroring means that stories create what researchers call "embodied cognition"—your brain processes narratives not as abstract information but as vicarious experience. When a customer reads about someone solving a problem with your product, their brain simulates the satisfaction of solving that problem themselves. When they encounter a story about someone achieving a goal that resonates with their own aspirations, their neural reward systems activate as if they were moving toward that achievement.

This explains why the most effective marketing often feels less like advertising and more like experiencing possibility. Great brand stories don't just tell customers what your product does—they let customers neurologically experience what their life might feel like with your product as part of it.

Mirror Neurons and Marketing Empathy

The discovery of mirror neurons in the 1990s revolutionized neuroscience's understanding of empathy and social connection. These specialized brain cells fire both when you perform an action and when you observe someone else performing the same action. They create automatic neurological empathy—when you watch someone smile, your mirror neurons fire as if you were smiling, often triggering an unconscious mimicking response and the associated positive feelings.

For marketers, mirror neurons explain why authentic testimonials and user-generated content can be so much more powerful than polished advertising claims. When potential customers see real people genuinely enjoying your product, having authentic emotional responses to your service, or solving actual problems with your solution, their mirror neurons fire in synchrony with those observed experiences.

But mirror neurons are sophisticated detection systems. They respond differently to authentic versus performed emotions, to genuine versus scripted interactions, to real versus fabricated scenarios. This is why focus-grouped marketing messages often feel hollow despite being technically well-crafted, and why unpolished but authentic customer stories can be more compelling than expensive production values.

Consider the difference between watching someone genuinely laugh at something funny versus watching an actor perform laughter on cue. Even when the performed laughter is technically perfect, your mirror neurons detect subtle differences in facial muscle activation, timing, and emotional authenticity. The same principle applies to marketing narratives: your audience's mirror neurons are constantly assessing whether the emotions and experiences in your stories seem genuine or contrived.

The Architecture of Compelling Narratives

Neuroscientific research reveals that effective stories follow patterns that align with how the brain naturally processes and remembers information. These patterns aren't arbitrary cultural conventions—they reflect the neurological architecture of human attention, emotion, and memory formation.

Narrative Arc and Neural Engagement: Stories that follow classic dramatic structure—setup, conflict, resolution—activate what neuroscientists call the "narrative network" in the brain. This network includes the medial prefrontal cortex (involved in understanding others' mental states), the posterior cingulate cortex (involved in self-referential thinking), and the temporal poles (involved in social and emotional processing). When these regions work together, they create what researchers term "transportation"—the experience of being fully immersed in a narrative world.

Emotional Peaks and Memory Formation: The brain's memory systems are designed to prioritize emotionally significant events. Stories that create emotional peaks—moments of tension, surprise, joy, or revelation—trigger the release of neurochemicals that enhance memory consolidation. This is why people remember stories long after they forget statistics, and why narrative-based marketing messages have longer-lasting impact than feature-and-benefit communications.

Character Identification and Self-Relevance: When story characters share traits, goals, or challenges with the audience, the brain's default mode network activates—the same neural system involved in self-referential thinking and imagining future scenarios. This creates what psychologists call "narrative transportation," where the boundary between self and story character becomes blurred at a neurological level.

The Oxytocin Connection

Paul Zak's research identified oxytocin as a key neurochemical mediator of story-driven influence. Often referred to as the "trust hormone," oxytocin is naturally released during positive social interactions, physical affection, and experiences of empathy and emotional connection. Stories that follow specific patterns can trigger the release of oxytocin in audiences, creating neurochemical states associated with trust, generosity, and social bonding.

The most effective oxytocin-triggering stories share several characteristics:

- **Character-driven rather than plot-driven**: The audience connects with a specific person facing relatable challenges
- **The emotional arc builds tension, then provides resolution**: The neurochemical reward comes from experiencing relief or satisfaction after the tension is resolved.
- **Clear demonstration of character change or growth**: The brain's reward systems respond to witnessing transformation
- **Authentic emotional expression**: Mirror neurons detect and respond to genuine rather than performed emotions

For marketers, this research suggests that the most influential brand stories are those that follow these neurologically optimized patterns while remaining authentic to real customer experiences. The goal isn't to manufacture emotional responses through narrative manipulation, but to identify and share genuine customer stories that naturally activate these neurological systems.

Beyond Features and Benefits: Emotional Narratives that Sell

Traditional marketing communication often follows a logical structure: problem identification, solution presentation, feature explanation, benefit articulation, and call to action. This approach assumes that customers make decisions through conscious evaluation of rational criteria. Neuroscience reveals a different reality: customers make most decisions emotionally and then use rational criteria to justify choices they've already made unconsciously.

This doesn't mean that features and benefits are irrelevant—it means they serve a different function than traditionally assumed. Rational information provides post-decision justification and conscious confidence in choices driven by emotional and neurological responses to narrative experiences.

The Neurological Sequence of Decision-Making

1. **Emotional Response** (immediate): Mirror neurons and emotional centers respond to story characters and situations, creating approach or avoidance impulses
2. **Social Validation** (rapid): The brain assesses whether the story represents experiences that align with the customer's identity and social context
3. **Future Simulation** (unconscious): The default mode network imagines what life might be like with this product or service integrated into personal experience
4. **Rational Justification** (conscious): The prefrontal cortex identifies logical reasons that support the emotionally driven preference

Effective marketing honors this sequence by leading with emotionally compelling narratives and supporting them with rational information, rather than attempting to persuade solely through logic.

The Authenticity Imperative

Perhaps the most important insight from neuroscientific research on storytelling is that authenticity isn't just an ethical preference—it's a neurological requirement for influence. The human brain has evolved sophisticated systems for detecting deception, inconsistency, and manipulation. These systems operate largely outside conscious awareness but generate powerful approach or avoidance responses.

When marketing stories are based on genuine customer experiences, when brand narratives align with actual company values and behaviors, when product claims match real performance, the brain's authenticity detection systems generate positive responses that support influence and persuasion. When stories feel manufactured, when brand positioning contradicts observable behavior, when promises exceed delivery, these same systems generate resistance that undermines even the most sophisticated marketing techniques.

This creates what we might call the "authenticity advantage": brands that build their narratives on genuine customer value and authentic experiences don't have to work as hard to create influence because their stories naturally align with neurological systems designed to detect and respond to truth.

Practical Applications: Story-Driven Marketing

Understanding the neuroscience of narrative provides practical guidance for creating more effective marketing communication:

Customer Story Collection: Instead of creating fictional scenarios or highly polished case studies, invest in identifying and sharing authentic customer stories that naturally follow emotionally compelling narrative arcs. Look for stories that include challenges, struggles, transformations, and genuine emotional responses.

Narrative Message Architecture: Structure marketing messages to engage the brain's narrative processing systems: establish a relatable character, introduce meaningful conflict or challenge, and provide satisfying resolution through your product or service. This applies whether you're crafting a 30-second commercial or a comprehensive content marketing campaign.

Emotional Authenticity: Ensure that any emotions displayed in your marketing—whether through photography, video, written tone, or spokesperson presentation—reflect genuine feelings rather than those that are performed. The brain's mirror neuron systems will detect and respond to authenticity or inauthenticity at levels below conscious awareness.

Character-Driven Content: Focus stories on specific individuals rather than abstract customer segments. The brain responds more powerfully to narratives about particular people facing concrete challenges than to generalized descriptions of target demographics solving hypothetical problems.

Transformation Emphasis: Highlight genuine change and growth in customer stories rather than just problem-solving or feature utilization. The brain's reward systems are particularly responsive to narratives that demonstrate meaningful transformation in a character's circumstances, capabilities, or well-being.

The Responsibility of Narrative Power

With the understanding that stories can literally change brain chemistry and influence behavior comes the responsibility to use this power ethically. The same neurological systems that respond to authentic, value-creating narratives can be exploited by manipulative storytelling designed to generate behavior that serves the marketer rather than the customer.

Ethical story-driven marketing:

- **Shares genuine customer experiences** rather than manufactured scenarios designed to trigger specific responses
- **Aligns narrative promises with actual delivery** rather than creating expectations that exceed product or service reality
- **Respects audience intelligence** rather than attempting to bypass conscious evaluation through emotional manipulation
- **Creates stories that serve customer needs** rather than exploiting neurological vulnerabilities for commercial gain

The goal is not to become more sophisticated at neurological manipulation, but to become more effective at authentic communication. When you understand how the brain processes stories, you can craft narratives that genuinely serve both your business objectives and your customers' actual needs and aspirations.

The Future of Story-Driven Influence

As neuroscientific research continues to reveal how narrative affects brain function, and as audiences become more sophisticated at detecting inauthentic communication, the brands that will thrive are those that master authentic story-driven marketing. This requires not only understanding the technical aspects of how stories work neurologically, but also developing the organizational capabilities to generate genuine customer value worth telling stories about consistently.

The most powerful marketing stories aren't crafted in conference rooms or focus groups—they emerge from authentic customer experiences with products and services that genuinely improve people's lives. When you create real value, authentic stories follow naturally. When those stories are shared in ways that honor both neurological realities and ethical principles, influence becomes a natural byproduct of service rather than a goal to be achieved through sophisticated persuasion techniques.

In the next chapter, we'll explore how the brain's reward systems create anticipation and desire, and how understanding dopamine pathways can help you design customer experiences that work with rather than against neurological realities.

Chapter 5

Dopamine, Anticipation, and Brand Lust

Reward pathways and brand engagement—Case: Apple's product launches & anticipation loops

At 12:01 AM Pacific Time on September 15, 2023, millions of people around the world simultaneously refreshed their browsers, opened mobile apps, and called phone numbers, all with the same urgent goal: to pre-order a device they had never physically touched, whose performance they had never personally tested, whose necessity in their lives was entirely hypothetical. The iPhone 15 had just become available for purchase.

Within the first hour, delivery estimates for premium models had stretched to six weeks. Social media is filled with screenshots of successful order confirmations, treated like lottery winnings. Professional adults took breaks from important meetings to check the status of their orders. The anticipation wasn't just for a phone—it was for the neurochemical reward of acquisition, the social satisfaction of early adoption, and the identity validation that came with being associated with a brand that had become synonymous with innovation and status.

This phenomenon reveals one of the most powerful forces in modern marketing: the deliberate activation of the brain's reward prediction systems to create what can only be described as brand lust. In this neurochemical state, desire for a product transcends rational evaluation of need or value.

The Neuroscience of Wanting

To understand how brands like Apple create such intense anticipation and desire, it is necessary to examine the brain's reward prediction system and its primary neurochemical mediator, dopamine. Popular culture often mischaracterizes dopamine as the "pleasure chemical," but neuroscientific research reveals a more sophisticated and marketing-relevant reality.

Dopamine doesn't create pleasure—it creates wanting. More precisely, it signals the predicted reward value of experiences and motivates behavior toward obtaining those rewards. The dopamine system evolved to help our ancestors pursue resources necessary for survival and reproduction. Still, in modern environments, it responds to a much broader range of stimuli, including brand experiences, product acquisitions, and social status signals.

The crucial insight for marketers is that dopamine release peaks not when you receive a reward, but when you anticipate receiving it. The neurochemical high comes from expecting something wonderful to happen, not from the wonderful thing actually happening. This explains why the most successful brands don't just create great products—they create exquisite anticipation for those products.

The Dopamine Cycle in Consumer Behavior

1. **Cue Recognition**: Environmental triggers signal potential reward availability (product launch announcement, sale notification, scarcity indicator)
2. **Anticipation Build**: Dopamine release increases as the brain predicts future reward
3. **Approach Behavior**: Neurochemical motivation drives action toward reward acquisition
4. **Outcome Evaluation**: Actual experience is compared to the predicted experience
5. **Learning Update**: The brain adjusts future reward predictions based on actual outcomes

Understanding this cycle reveals why traditional marketing approaches often fail: they focus on step 4 (outcome) while ignoring the much more neurochemically powerful steps 2 and 3 (anticipation and approach).

The Neurobiology of Brand Anticipation

When brands successfully activate dopamine pathways, they create what neuroscientists call "incentive salience"—the psychological state in which obtaining something becomes compellingly important, regardless of its objective utility. This explains why people camp outside stores for product launches, refresh websites obsessively during limited releases, or genuinely feel excited about delivery notifications.

Apple has become the master case study in dopamine-driven marketing. Still, its approach isn't manipulative trickery—it's a systematic understanding of how anticipation works neurologically, combined with consistent delivery of experiences that validate and reinforce that anticipation.

Apple's Dopamine Architecture

Predictable Unpredictability: Apple creates anticipation through reliable timing (September events, predictable release cycles) combined with genuine uncertainty about specific features and capabilities. The brain's reward system responds powerfully to situations where reward is likely but details remain unknown.

Scarcity and Social Proof: Limited initial availability creates a sense of urgency, while social media amplification provides social validation for the desire. The combination activates both individual reward circuits and social status systems simultaneously.

Progressive Revelation: Instead of revealing everything at once, Apple parcels out information through carefully orchestrated leaks, rumors, keynote presentations, and hands-on opportunities. Each revelation triggers a new wave of dopamine release as anticipated features become confirmed realities.

Ritual and Community: The entire launch process becomes a shared cultural experience with its own rituals, language, and community dynamics. Participating in the anticipation becomes socially rewarding independent of the product itself.

Consistent Over-Delivery: Perhaps most importantly, Apple products typically meet or exceed the expectations created during the anticipation period. This validates the brain's reward predictions and strengthens future dopamine responses to stimuli associated with Apple.

The Psychology of Scarcity and Exclusivity

Scarcity triggers what behavioral economists call "loss aversion"—the tendency to feel potential losses more intensely than equivalent potential gains. However, neuroscience reveals a more complex dynamic: scarcity doesn't just create a fear of missing out; it amplifies the perceived reward value of whatever is scarce.

When the brain perceives that something desirable might not be available, dopamine systems interpret this as increased reward value. The anticipation becomes more intense, the motivation stronger, and the satisfaction of eventual acquisition greater. This isn't irrational behavior—it's the appropriate neurological response to environments where valuable resources are genuinely limited.

The challenge for marketers is distinguishing between authentic scarcity, which reflects genuine limitations, and artificial scarcity, designed purely to manipulate dopamine responses. The difference matters both ethically and practically, because sophisticated consumers increasingly recognize and resist manufactured urgency while still responding powerfully to authentic limited availability.

Authentic Scarcity

- Limited production capacity or seasonal availability
- Genuine time constraints around special offers or access
- Natural exclusivity based on skill, commitment, or qualification requirements
- Real social limitations around community size or intimate experiences

Manufactured Scarcity

- Arbitrary quantity limits unrelated to actual constraints
- Fake countdown timers and manufactured urgency
- Artificial exclusivity designed to create status anxiety
- Repeated "limited time" offers that undermine their own credibility

Variable Ratio Reinforcement and Engagement

Some of the most psychologically compelling anticipation loops employ what behavioral psychologists call "variable ratio reinforcement"—reward schedules where the timing or magnitude of rewards varies unpredictably. This creates higher levels of engagement and motivation than fixed, predictable reward patterns.

Social media platforms have built their engagement systems around variable ratio reinforcement: you never know when you'll receive a like, comment, or share that triggers your social reward systems. Email marketing often employs similar principles: newsletters that sometimes contain valuable content and sometimes don't, flash sales that happen at unpredictable intervals, loyalty programs that randomly offer bonus rewards.

The key insight is that uncertainty about reward timing and magnitude increases rather than decreases engagement, provided that rewards do occur frequently enough to maintain motivation. The brain finds variable ratio schedules more compelling than either constant reward or constant non-reward.

For brand building, consistent value delivery should be combined with unpredictable bonus experiences. Customers should know they can rely on your core offering while remaining delightfully uncertain about when you might exceed their expectations.

The Dark Side of Dopamine Marketing

The power of dopamine-driven marketing creates significant ethical responsibilities. The same neurological systems that create healthy motivation and goal pursuit can be exploited to generate compulsive behavior that serves marketers rather than customers. Understanding how anticipation and reward systems work neurologically requires an accompanying understanding of when their activation becomes manipulation rather than service.

Problematic Applications

- **Addiction-Adjacent Design:** Creating engagement patterns that mirror addictive substances or behaviors
- **Exploitation of Vulnerability:** Targeting dopamine systems in people struggling with impulse control, financial limitations, or psychological vulnerabilities
- **Infinite Treadmill:** Designing experiences where satisfaction is permanently deferred in favor of continuous anticipation
- **Identity Manipulation:** Using reward systems to make people feel that their self-worth depends on consumption patterns or brand affiliations

Ethical Applications

- **Value-First Anticipation:** Creating excitement for products and services that genuinely improve customer lives
- **Sustainable Engagement:** Designing reward systems that enhance rather than replace intrinsic motivation
- **Authentic Community:** Building anticipation around shared values and experiences rather than just acquisition
- **Long-term Satisfaction:** Ensuring that actual experiences meet or exceed the anticipation created during marketing

Building Healthy Anticipation Loops

The goal isn't to avoid activating customer reward systems—motivation and anticipation are natural, healthy aspects of human psychology. The goal is to activate these systems in ways that serve genuine customer interests while building sustainable business relationships.

Anticipation for Value Creation: Generate excitement for products, services, or experiences that will genuinely improve customer lives. The anticipation should be proportional to the actual benefit the customer will receive.

Community-Centered Scarcity: When creating limited availability, prioritize preserving the quality of the customer experience over creating artificial urgency. Limited workshop sizes that ensure personal attention, seasonal offerings that reflect actual production constraints, or exclusive access that creates genuine community value.

Progressive Value Revelation: Instead of revealing everything at once, unfold your value proposition over time in ways that build understanding and appreciation. This might involve educational content that prepares customers for new offerings, behind-the-scenes access that fosters an appreciation for your process, or staged releases that allow customers to fully absorb and benefit from each element.

Surprise and Delight Systems: Create unpredictable positive experiences for existing customers rather than focusing all anticipation-building on acquisition. Unexpected upgrades, bonus content, or personalized touches that reward loyalty and create positive anticipation for future interactions.

Transparent Communication: Be honest about availability, timing, and what customers can realistically expect. Authentic anticipation is more sustainable than manufactured hype because it builds trust rather than eroding it.

Case Study: Beyond Apple - Diverse Approaches to Anticipation

While Apple represents perhaps the most sophisticated approach to dopamine-driven marketing, other brands demonstrate that anticipation can be built in ways that align with different values and customer relationships.

Patagonia creates anticipation around environmental impact and seasonal adventures rather than product acquisition. Their "Don't Buy This Jacket" campaign generated massive engagement by creating anticipation for participating in environmental consciousness rather than consumption.

Tesla builds anticipation around technological advancement and sustainable transportation rather than just vehicle ownership. Their approach fosters a community centered on shared values and a shared vision for the future, rather than just product desire.

Nintendo generates anticipation through gameplay revelation and community discovery rather than just hardware launches. Their approach builds excitement for experiences and social connection rather than just acquisition.

Each approach activates dopamine systems but channels that activation toward different types of rewards: environmental contribution, technological progress, creative expression, and social connection. The neurological mechanisms are similar, but the outcomes serve broader customer interests beyond immediate consumption.

The Future of Ethical Anticipation Marketing

As understanding of neurological reward systems becomes more widespread, both among marketers and consumers, the brands that will thrive are those that use this knowledge to create genuine value rather than exploit psychological vulnerabilities. Consumers are becoming increasingly sophisticated at recognizing and resisting manipulative anticipation tactics while still responding powerfully to authentic excitement about valuable offerings.

The future belongs to brands that can create what we might call "conscious anticipation"—neurochemical engagement that customers understand and welcome because it points toward experiences they genuinely want and value.

This requires transparency about marketing techniques, honesty about product limitations, and commitment to delivering experiences that justify the anticipation created around them.

When dopamine-driven marketing is grounded in authentic value creation and ethical principles, it becomes a powerful tool for building sustainable customer relationships rather than extracting short-term profit from neurological vulnerabilities. The anticipation becomes genuinely collaborative—brands and customers working together to create experiences worth looking forward to.

In our next chapter, we'll explore how memory and cognitive biases influence customer decision-making, and how understanding these mental mechanisms can help create marketing that works with, rather than against, the brain's natural information processing systems.

Chapter 6

Memory, Bias, and Recall

How the brain encodes brands—anchoring, availability bias, and creating "sticky" messages

Consider this question: How much would you pay for a high-quality winter coat? Before you answer, think about this number: 1,247. Now, how much would you pay for that same coat?

If you're like most people, the random number 1,247 just influenced your pricing estimate, even though it has absolutely nothing to do with coats, winter gear, or anything else relevant to your decision. This demonstrates one of the most powerful and pervasive forces shaping consumer behavior: the brain's reliance on cognitive shortcuts that can be systematically influenced by seemingly irrelevant information.

This phenomenon, known as anchoring bias, represents just one of dozens of mental mechanisms that determine how customers remember your brand, evaluate your offerings, and make purchasing decisions. Understanding these mechanisms isn't about exploiting psychological vulnerabilities—it's about designing marketing that works with rather than against the brain's natural information processing systems.

For marketers, the implications are profound: your customers' memories of your brand aren't accurate recordings of their experiences with you. They're reconstructions shaped by neurological biases, influenced by contextual factors, and filtered through cognitive shortcuts that evolved to help humans make rapid decisions in environments very different from modern markets.

The Architecture of Brand Memory

Memory isn't a filing cabinet where experiences are stored intact for later retrieval. It's a dynamic reconstruction system that rebuilds experiences each time they're recalled, influenced by current context, emotional state, subsequent experiences, and cognitive biases operating outside conscious awareness.

When customers remember your brand, they're not accessing stored files of their interactions with you. They're reconstructing those experiences using fragments of actual memory combined with assumptions, expectations, and mental shortcuts. This reconstruction process is vulnerable to systematic biases that can work either for or against your marketing objectives.

Three Memory Systems Relevant to Marketing

Working Memory holds immediate conscious awareness—the brand names, product features, and marketing messages currently in active consideration. This system has extremely limited capacity (roughly 7±2 items) and brief duration (15-30 seconds without rehearsal), making it the most competitive arena for marketing attention.

Long-term Explicit Memory stores consciously accessible information about brand experiences, product features, and marketing messages. This system has a vast capacity, but it requires effortful encoding and retrieval, making memorable marketing a significant challenge in information-rich environments.

Long-term Implicit Memory encompasses unconscious associations, emotional responses, and procedural knowledge related to brands. This system operates automatically and influences decision-making without conscious awareness, making it the most important but least understood target for brand building.

The most successful brands don't just compete for conscious attention—they systematically build positive implicit associations that influence choice behavior even when customers aren't consciously thinking about the brand.

The Anchoring Effect in Brand Positioning

The number 1,247 in our opening example illustrates the anchoring bias—the tendency for initial information to influence subsequent judgments disproportionately. In marketing contexts, anchoring operates continuously and powerfully, shaping how customers evaluate prices, assess quality, and compare options.

Price Anchoring: The first price customers encounter for a product category establishes an unconscious reference point that influences all subsequent price evaluations. This is why luxury brands often lead with their highest-priced offerings, why retailers display "original prices" alongside sale prices, and why subscription services emphasize annual costs over monthly ones.

Quality Anchoring: Initial brand encounters create lasting impressions that influence the interpretation of subsequent experiences. A customer's first interaction with your brand—whether through advertising, website experience, customer service, or product trial—sets the stage for quality expectations that shape their perception of all future interactions.

Category Anchoring: The first brand customers encounter in a new product category often becomes the unconscious standard against which all others are measured. This creates a significant advantage for category pioneers, explaining why being "first" can be more valuable than being "best."

Understanding anchoring allows marketers to deliberately establish favorable reference points rather than leaving these crucial first impressions to chance. But it also reveals why recovering from negative initial impressions requires more than just improving subsequent experiences—it requires actively resetting anchored expectations.

Availability Bias and Brand Salience

Availability bias refers to the tendency to judge the probability and importance of events based on how easily relevant examples come to mind. If you can quickly remember instances of something happening, you unconsciously assume it happens frequently or represents a typical experience. For brands, this creates both opportunities and vulnerabilities.

Media Coverage Amplification: Brands that receive frequent media attention—whether positive or negative—become more "available" in customer memory, increasing their perceived importance and influence. This explains why publicity can be more valuable than advertising, and why crisis management requires rapid response to prevent negative examples from becoming cognitively available.

Customer Experience Recency: Recent experiences with your brand are more cognitively available than older ones, making them disproportionately influential in overall brand perception. A single negative recent interaction can overshadow months of positive history because it's more mentally accessible when customers evaluate their relationship with your brand.

Social Proof Availability: Customers judge how satisfied other people are with your brand based on how easily they can remember examples of positive or negative experiences. This is why authentic testimonials, case studies, and user-generated content are so powerful—they make positive experiences more cognitively available.

Category Association: When customers think about your product category, which brands come to mind first? This "top-of-mind awareness" isn't just about recall—it's about which brands feel most relevant and important because they're most cognitively available when the need arises.

The Peak-End Rule and Experience Design

Nobel laureate Daniel Kahneman discovered that people remember experiences primarily based on two key moments: the peak (the most intense moment) and the end (the final moment). The duration of the experience and the average quality throughout have surprisingly little impact on memory and subsequent evaluation.

This "peak-end rule" has profound implications for customer experience design. Customers don't remember the total value they received from your brand—they remember how they felt during the most intense moment and how they felt when the interaction concluded.

Designing Memorable Peaks: Instead of trying to maintain consistent quality throughout every interaction, focus on creating specific moments of exceptional value, surprise, or delight. These peaks become disproportionately influential in overall brand memory.

Crafting Strong Endings: The final moments of customer interactions—such as purchase completion, product delivery, customer service resolution, or subscription cancellation—have an outsized impact on brand memory because they're both peak moments and ending moments simultaneously.

Managing Negative Peaks: When problems occur, focus on creating positive resolution experiences rather than just solving the immediate issue. The customer's memory will be shaped more by how the problem was resolved than by the fact that a problem occurred.

This research suggests that moderate, consistent experiences may be less memorable and influential than those that include both routine moments and exceptional peaks, provided the peaks are positive and the endings are strong.

Confirmation Bias and Brand Loyalty

Once customers form opinions about your brand, confirmation bias causes them to preferentially notice and remember information that supports their existing beliefs while ignoring or forgetting contradictory evidence. This creates both loyalty lock-in for satisfied customers and resistance to change among dissatisfied ones.

Positive Confirmation Loops: Customers who have a positive initial experience with your brand tend to notice and remember subsequent positive experiences while mentally minimizing negative ones. This creates increasingly strong brand preference over time, even when competitive offerings might be objectively superior.

Negative Confirmation Spirals: Customers who have a negative initial experience tend to notice and remember subsequent problems while mentally downplaying positive experiences. Recovering from a negative first impression requires not just improvement, but a deliberate pattern interruption that forces a conscious reevaluation.

Expectation Fulfillment: Customers often experience what they expect to experience, regardless of objective reality. Strong brand positioning creates expectations that influence perception of actual product or service performance.

Understanding confirmation bias suggests that initial brand experiences are disproportionately important, but also that consistent positive experiences compound their impact over time, while inconsistent experiences create cognitive dissonance that customers resolve by either becoming more loyal or completely disengaging.

The Halo Effect and Brand Extensions

The halo effect describes the tendency for impressions in one area to influence opinions in unrelated areas. If customers believe your brand is innovative, they tend to perceive your products as higher quality, your customer service as more helpful, and your company as more trustworthy, even without specific evidence to support these judgments.

Brand Attribute Transfer: Positive associations with your brand in one dimension (quality, innovation, trustworthiness, status) automatically transfer to other dimensions in customer perception. This allows strong brands to extend into new categories and charge premium prices across their entire portfolio.

Category Halo Effects: Success in one product category creates positive assumptions about performance in related categories. Apple's success with iPods created positive expectations for iPhones, which created positive expectations for iPads, and so on.

Experience Generalization: Exceptional performance in one area of customer experience creates positive assumptions about other areas. Outstanding customer service makes products seem higher quality; innovative product design makes customer service seem more responsive.

The halo effect explains why focused brand building—becoming exceptionally strong in one area before expanding—can be more effective than trying to be moderately good at everything simultaneously.

Creating "Sticky" Messages through Cognitive Alignment

Understanding memory and bias allows marketers to design messages that naturally align with how the brain processes and retains information. Instead of fighting against cognitive biases, effective marketing works with these mental shortcuts to create genuinely memorable and influential communication.

Simplicity and Cognitive Load: The limited capacity of working memory means that simple, clear messages are more likely to be encoded and retained than complex, information-dense communications. This doesn't mean dumbing down your marketing—it means distilling complex value propositions into cognitively manageable components.

Concrete over Abstract: The brain encodes specific, sensory-rich information more effectively than abstract concepts. "Removes 99.9% of bacteria" is more memorable than "highly effective sanitization"; "delivered in 30 minutes" is stickier than "fast delivery."

Story-Enhanced Encoding: As we explored in Chapter 4, narrative structure enhances memory formation by engaging multiple brain systems simultaneously. Information embedded in stories is more likely to be encoded, retained, and accurately recalled than information presented as isolated facts.

Emotional Tagging: Emotional experiences trigger the release of neurochemicals that enhance memory consolidation. Marketing messages that create genuine emotional responses—such as surprise, delight, inspiration, or even productive tension—are more likely to be remembered than emotionally neutral communications.

Repetition with Variation: While simple repetition can enhance memory, varied repetition—presenting the same core message through different formats, contexts, or examples—creates more robust memory encoding while avoiding habituation effects.

The Serial Position Effect in Message Architecture

People remember information from the beginning and end of sequences better than information from the middle. This "serial position effect" has direct implications for the structure of marketing messages.

Primacy Effect: The first information customers encounter about your brand has a disproportionate influence on overall impression and subsequent information processing. This makes opening statements, homepage headlines, and initial brand encounters critically important.

Recency Effect: The last information customers encounter before making a decision is disproportionately influential. This makes closing arguments, final calls to action, and last-minute communications particularly powerful.

Middle Message Management: Information presented in the middle of sequences is most vulnerable to forgetting. If you must include important but less compelling information, support it with visual emphasis, emotional resonance, or story structure to enhance memorability.

Understanding serial position effects suggests that message architecture should strategically place the most important information at the beginning and end positions while using special techniques to ensure middle content receives adequate attention and encoding.

The Illusion of Truth Effect

Repeated exposure to information increases perceived truthfulness, regardless of actual accuracy. This "illusory truth effect" occurs because familiar information is processed more fluently, and the brain interprets processing fluency as a signal of truth.

For marketers, this research has both positive applications and ethical implications:

Positive Applications

- Consistent brand messaging across channels increases perceived credibility
- Repeated exposure to value propositions enhances customer confidence
- Familiar brand associations feel more trustworthy and reliable

Ethical Considerations

- Repetition alone cannot make false claims true or ethical
- Customers develop sophisticated detection systems for manufactured familiarity
- Long-term brand trust requires that repeated messages align with experience

The illusion of truth effect suggests that consistent, honest messaging compounds its impact over time, while inconsistent or misleading communication ultimately undermines credibility despite short-term familiarity effects.

Practical Applications: Memory-Optimized Marketing

Understanding how memory and bias actually work provides concrete guidance for creating more effective marketing:

Anchor Strategically: Deliberately establish favorable reference points through pricing presentation, quality demonstrations, and competitive comparisons. Don't leave anchoring to chance.

Design for Peak-End: Focus customer experience design on creating memorable peaks and strong endings rather than trying to optimize every moment equally.

Build Cognitive Availability: Make positive brand associations easily accessible through storytelling, social proof, and consistent positive messaging across multiple touchpoints.

Align with Confirmation Tendencies: Understand existing customer beliefs and design experiences that allow positive confirmation while providing opportunities for negative belief revision.

Leverage Halo Effects: Build exceptional strength in one area before expanding, allowing positive associations to transfer to new offerings and categories.

Structure for Serial Position: Place your most important messages at the beginning and end of communications, using special techniques to ensure the middle content receives adequate attention.

The Responsibility of Memory Influence

With the understanding that marketing systematically influences memory formation and recall comes the responsibility to use this influence ethically. The same mechanisms that can help customers remember genuine value can be exploited to create false impressions or manipulative associations.

Ethical Memory-based Marketing

- **Aligns repeated messages with actual brand reality** rather than creating illusory truth through repetition alone
- **Creates memorable experiences based on genuine value delivery** rather than manufactured peaks designed to mask overall mediocrity
- **Uses anchoring to establish fair comparisons** rather than manipulating reference points to justify poor value
- **Builds positive associations that reflect authentic brand qualities** rather than creating halo effects that mask fundamental deficiencies

The goal is not to become more sophisticated at memory manipulation, but to understand how memory works so your authentic brand value is more likely to be accurately encoded, retained, and recalled by customers.

Toward Memory-Conscious Brand Building

As research continues to reveal how memory and bias shape customer behavior, the brands that will thrive are those that design their entire customer experience around how memory actually works rather than how we assume it works.

This means creating brands that are not just good, but memorably good in ways that align with neurological reality. It means designing customer interactions that naturally encode positive associations rather than leaving memory formation to chance. It means building marketing systems that work with cognitive biases rather than fighting against them.

When marketing is designed around an authentic understanding of memory and bias, it becomes more effective not by manipulating psychological vulnerabilities but by ensuring that genuine brand value is accurately represented in customer memory. The biases become allies in the service of truth rather than obstacles to overcome or weapons to exploit.

This completes our exploration of the neuroscience of influence. In Part III, we'll examine how these insights translate into practical strategies for creating marketing campaigns that consistently win both attention and hearts by working with rather than against the psychological realities we've discovered.

PART III: THE PSYCHOLOGY OF WINNING CAMPAIGNS

Part III

The Psychology of Winning Campaigns

In Parts I and II, we've journeyed through the inner landscape of marketing consciousness and the neurological terrain of human influence. We've discovered how your own cognitive architecture either supports or sabotages your creative work, explored how stories literally change brain chemistry, and examined how memory and bias shape customer perception in ways that most marketing education never addresses.

Now comes the essential translation: How do these insights transform from fascinating knowledge into winning campaigns? How do you bridge the gap between understanding how minds work and creating marketing that consistently captures attention, builds genuine connection, and drives meaningful action?

Part III addresses this challenge by examining the psychology of campaigns that break through the noise, resonate authentically with their intended audiences, and achieve both commercial success and cultural impact. But this isn't simply a collection of tactical best practices or case study analyses. Instead, we'll explore how the most successful campaigns emerge from deep integration of the principles we've established: conscious-unconscious collaboration in the marketer, neurological resonance with the audience, and authentic value creation that serves both business objectives and genuine human needs.

The Attention Paradox

We live in what economist Herbert Simon first called "the attention economy"—an environment where information is abundant but human attention is the scarce resource. The average person encounters between 3,000 and 5,000 marketing messages daily, yet consciously processes only a tiny fraction of them. Most marketing, no matter how cleverly crafted or expensively produced, simply disappears into the background noise of modern life.

This creates what we might call the attention paradox: the harder marketers try to capture attention through traditional means—louder messages, brighter visuals, more frequent contact, more urgent language—the more sophisticated consumers become at filtering out these attempts. The very effort to break through the noise often contributes to making it worse.

Yet certain campaigns cut through this din effortlessly, creating what feels like spontaneous cultural moments where suddenly everyone is talking about a brand, sharing a message, or engaging with content. These breakthrough campaigns don't seem to fight for attention—they seem to attract it naturally, as if the audience was already looking for exactly what the campaign offered.

The difference lies in understanding attention not as something to be captured or stolen, but as something to be earned through genuine relevance to the psychological and neurological realities we've explored. Winning campaigns don't just interrupt the flow of attention—they become part of it, aligning so naturally with how minds actually work that engagement feels inevitable rather than effortful.

Beyond Persuasion: The Resonance Model

Traditional marketing operates on what we might call the "persuasion model"—the assumption that customers have existing preferences that must be overcome through strategic argument, emotional manipulation, or incentive structures. This model treats customer resistance as a problem to be solved through more sophisticated persuasion techniques.

But the neuroscientific insights we've explored suggest a fundamentally different approach: the "resonance model." Instead of trying to change customer preferences, resonant marketing identifies and amplifies preferences that already exist but may not be fully conscious or clearly articulated. Instead of overcoming resistance, it eliminates resistance by aligning so closely with existing psychological realities that adoption feels natural rather than persuaded.

Consider the difference between a campaign that argues "you should want this" versus one that helps customers recognize "you already want this, you just didn't know it yet." The first requires overcoming psychological resistance; the second eliminates resistance by activating existing but unexpressed desires.

This shift from persuasion to resonance changes everything about how campaigns are conceived, developed, and executed. Instead of starting with what you want customers to believe or do, you start with deep understanding of what they already believe, feel, and aspire to. Instead of crafting arguments to change minds, you create experiences that reveal minds to themselves.

The Neurology of Cultural Moments

The most successful campaigns don't just reach individual customers—they create what sociologists call "cultural moments," where brand messages become part of broader social conversations. These moments feel organic and spontaneous, but they emerge from systematic understanding of how ideas spread through social networks and become embedded in collective consciousness.

Neuroscientific research reveals that viral content and cultural phenomena follow predictable patterns based on how human brains process social information. We're wired to pay special attention to information that seems relevant to our social status, identity, and group membership. We're neurologically programmed to share content that makes us look smart, caring, or connected to our social networks.

Winning campaigns understand these social psychological realities and design content that naturally activates sharing behaviors not through artificial incentives or manipulative triggers, but by creating genuine value for both the sharer and their social network. The campaign becomes socially useful—something people actually want to share because it serves their relationships and their identity.

This social amplification isn't just about reaching more people—it's about reaching them through trusted sources with implicit social endorsement. When someone you respect shares a brand message, your brain processes it differently than when you encounter that same message through paid advertising. The neurological pathways for social proof and authority combine to create receptiveness that no amount of paid media can replicate.

The Integration Challenge

Perhaps the greatest challenge facing modern marketers is integration—not just across channels and touchpoints, but across the psychological realities we've explored. How do you create campaigns that simultaneously honor your own creative intuition and analytical rigor? How do you design experiences that activate customer reward systems while building genuine trust? How do you craft messages that are both memorable and authentic, both socially shareable and personally meaningful?

The answer lies in what we might call "psychological integration"—designing campaigns where every element supports and reinforces every other element at multiple levels of consciousness. The rational content supports the emotional experience. The visual design aligns with the neurological impact. The distribution strategy reflects the social psychology. The measurement systems capture both conscious responses and unconscious influence.

This integration can't be achieved through checklists or formulas because it requires the kind of intuitive understanding that emerges from deep familiarity with both the principles we've explored and the specific context of your brand, audience, and market dynamics. It's more like learning to play jazz than following a recipe—improvisation guided by thorough knowledge of underlying structures.

The Three Pillars of Winning Campaigns

Through analysis of campaigns that have achieved both commercial success and cultural impact, three consistent patterns emerge—what we might call the three pillars of winning campaigns:

Attention Architecture: Instead of fighting for attention, these campaigns create experiences that naturally align with how attention actually works neurologically and psychologically. They understand the difference between interruption and invitation, between capture and attraction.

Authentic Performance: These campaigns achieve the paradoxical balance of being strategically optimized while feeling completely natural and uncontrived. They perform authentically rather than authentically performing—a distinction that audiences detect unconsciously but powerfully.

Confidence Resonance: Perhaps most importantly, these campaigns emerge from genuine confidence in the value being offered. This confidence is neurologically transmitted to audiences through subtle cues that operate below conscious awareness but above the level of mere technique.

The Evolution of Marketing Mastery

The campaigns we'll examine in Part III represent an evolution in marketing sophistication—not toward more complex tactics or advanced technologies, but toward deeper integration of psychological understanding with authentic value creation. They demonstrate what becomes possible when marketers master their own inner game while simultaneously understanding the neurological realities of their audiences.

This mastery isn't achieved through additional techniques or more sophisticated tools, but through what we might call "conscious competence"—the ability to operate from both analytical understanding and intuitive wisdom while remaining fully present to the unique requirements of each campaign challenge.

The most successful marketers of the next decade will be those who can fluidly integrate logical analysis with creative insight, who understand both spreadsheets and stories, who can optimize for metrics while preserving meaning. They'll create campaigns that feel effortless to experience but emerge from a deep understanding of the psychological principles that govern all human communication and influence.

Beyond Winning: The Service Model

As we examine winning campaigns, it's important to remember that the ultimate goal isn't just commercial success—it's contributing to a marketing ecosystem that genuinely serves human needs and aspirations. The most sustainable competitive advantage comes not from being more sophisticated at psychological manipulation, but from being more authentic in psychological service.

The campaigns that achieve lasting impact are those that win not just customer attention and preference, but customer gratitude. They don't just succeed in their immediate commercial objectives—they leave audiences feeling better about themselves, more optimistic about their possibilities, or more connected to what matters most to them.

This service orientation doesn't diminish commercial effectiveness—it enhances it by creating the kind of authentic value that generates sustainable competitive advantage. When customers feel genuinely served by your marketing, they become not just buyers but advocates, not just audiences but collaborators in your brand's success.

The Art of Psychological Aikido

Perhaps the best metaphor for the approach we'll explore in Part III is aikido. This martial art achieves maximum effectiveness through minimum effort by working with rather than against opposing forces. Psychological aikido in marketing involves understanding the existing forces in customer consciousness—their desires, fears, social pressures, and neurological patterns—and designing campaigns that redirect these forces toward mutual benefit, rather than trying to overcome them through superior force.

This requires a fundamental shift in mindset: from seeing customer psychology as something to be conquered to seeing it as something to be honored, from viewing resistance as a problem to be solved to viewing it as information about misalignment to be corrected, from approaching campaigns as battles to be won to approaching them as dances to be performed.

When marketing achieves this psychological aikido, something remarkable happens: success becomes effortless, not because it requires no effort, but because the effort is perfectly aligned with natural psychological and neurological realities. The campaign works because it inherently honors rather than violates the fundamental principles governing how minds connect, communicate, and change.

Welcome to the psychology of winning campaigns, where victory emerges not from superior force but from superior understanding, not from more sophisticated manipulation but from more authentic service, not from fighting against the human mind but from dancing with it in ways that serve both marketer and audience equally.

Chapter 7

The Inner Game of Attention

Competing in the economy of distraction—peak attention strategies (Nike, TikTok virality)

On September 5, 2018, Nike made a decision that would define not just their brand but the entire conversation around corporate activism for years to come. In a simple black-and-white advertisement featuring Colin Kaepernick, they displayed four words that instantly divided the internet, sparked international debate, and generated an estimated $6 billion in brand value: "Believe in something. Even if it means sacrificing everything."

Within hours, the campaign had achieved something that most marketers spend millions trying to accomplish: complete cultural penetration. It dominated social media feeds, cable news broadcasts, dinner table conversations, and workplace discussions. Nike's stock price initially dropped, then soared to record highs. The company received both passionate support and fierce criticism, but perhaps most importantly, they had achieved something increasingly rare in the attention economy: they had made indifference impossible.

This wasn't just successful advertising—it was masterful attention architecture. Nike understood something profound about how attention actually works in the modern media landscape: the opposite of attention isn't distraction, it's apathy. And the path to capturing genuine attention isn't through louder, brighter, or more frequent messaging—it's through creating content so aligned with existing psychological tensions that engagement becomes inevitable.

The Neuroscience of Attention Selection

To understand how campaigns like Nike's breakthrough while thousands of others disappear into digital noise, we need to examine what neuroscientists have discovered about attention selection. This is the largely unconscious process by which the brain decides what deserves conscious awareness from the overwhelming flood of available information.

The human brain processes approximately 11 million bits of information per second, but conscious awareness can handle only about 40 bits per second. This means that 99.9996% of available information never reaches conscious attention. The brain's filtering systems aren't just important—they're essential for psychological survival in information-rich environments.

These attention filters operate according to predictable criteria that evolved to help our ancestors survive in very different environments, but still govern modern attention allocation:

Novelty Detection: The brain prioritizes information that's different from established patterns. But true novelty is rare—most "new" marketing messages are variations on familiar themes. The attention advantage goes to content that combines familiar elements in genuinely unexpected ways.

Threat and Opportunity Assessment: Information that suggests either danger or significant opportunity receives priority processing. This explains why negative news spreads faster than positive news, but also why genuinely transformative opportunities can capture attention despite being positive.

Social Relevance Evaluation: The brain automatically assesses whether information might affect social status, group membership, or relationships. Content that helps people signal their identity, values, or affiliations naturally receives enhanced attention.

Personal Significance Scanning: Information that seems directly relevant to individual goals, challenges, or identity receives preferential processing. This isn't just about demographic targeting—it's about psychological relevance.

Nike's Kaepernick campaign succeeded because it activated all four attention selection criteria simultaneously: it was genuinely novel in corporate communications, presented both threat and opportunity depending on perspective, was intensely socially relevant in the cultural moment, and demanded personal stance-taking from viewers.

The Paradox of Trying Too Hard

Perhaps the most counterintuitive insight from attention research is that the harder brands try to capture attention through traditional means—brighter colors, louder volume, more urgent language, increased frequency—the more sophisticated audiences become at filtering out these attempts. The human brain is remarkably good at detecting and dismissing what neuroscientists call "intentional influence attempts."

When marketing messages feel obviously designed to capture attention, influence behavior, or manipulate responses, the brain's defensive systems activate, creating resistance rather than engagement. This explains why traditional interruption-based advertising is becoming less effective while content that feels organic, authentic, or user-generated can achieve viral spread with minimal promotional support.

The Effort Paradox in Action

- **High Effort, Low Impact:** Campaigns that obviously strain for attention often achieve high exposure but low engagement
- **Low Effort, High Impact:** Content that feels effortless often generates spontaneous sharing and extended engagement
- **Authenticity Detection:** Audiences unconsciously distinguish between genuine and manufactured authenticity with remarkable accuracy
- **Resistance Generation:** Obvious persuasion attempts often create psychological reactance—the opposite of the intended response

This doesn't mean that successful campaigns require no effort—it means that the effort must be invisible to the audience, channeled into understanding and serving their psychological needs rather than overcoming their resistance.

TikTok and the Algorithm of Unconscious Engagement

TikTok's explosive growth from startup to cultural phenomenon provides perhaps the most instructive case study in modern attention capture. The platform didn't succeed through superior technology or marketing budget—it succeeded by creating an algorithm that operates according to the same principles as human attention selection, amplifying content that naturally aligns with neurological engagement patterns.

TikTok's Attention Architecture

Micro-Novelty: The platform's short-form format creates continuous novelty without requiring sustained attention investment. Each video represents a complete novelty cycle—setup, development, resolution—in 15-60 seconds.

Emotional Intensity: The algorithm prioritizes content that generates strong emotional responses—laughter, surprise, outrage, inspiration—because these trigger the neurochemical states associated with memory formation and sharing behavior.

Social Proof Integration: The interface makes engagement visible and immediate, activating social proof mechanisms that influence how subsequent viewers allocate their attention and respond.

Personalization Without Obvious Targeting: The recommendation system feels like discovery rather than targeting, avoiding the resistance that comes with obvious algorithmic manipulation.

Participation Invitation: Unlike passive consumption platforms, TikTok consistently invites users to create rather than consume, transforming attention from resource extraction to collaborative creation.

For marketers, TikTok's success reveals that winning attention strategies must work with rather than against the brain's natural engagement patterns. The most successful TikTok marketing doesn't feel like marketing—it feels like entertainment, education, or social connection that happens to involve brands.

Peak Attention States: Flow and Focus

Neuroscientist Mihaly Csikszentmihalyi's research on flow states reveals that peak attention engagement occurs when challenge and skill are perfectly matched, when self-consciousness disappears, and when the activity becomes intrinsically rewarding. While flow states typically describe individual experiences, similar principles apply to marketing content that achieves sustained audience engagement.

Marketing Flow States

- **Optimal Challenge:** Content that's neither too simple (boring) nor too complex (overwhelming) but perfectly calibrated to audience sophistication
- **Clear Objectives:** Messages where the purpose and value are immediately apparent without being heavy-handed
- **Immediate Feedback:** Interactive elements that provide instant response to audience engagement

- **Merged Action-Awareness:** Content so engaging that the boundary between marketer and audience dissolves into a collaborative experience

Nike's most successful campaigns often achieve these flow-like states. Their "Just Do It" messaging provides optimal challenge (encouraging action without prescribing specific behaviors), clear objectives (overcome internal resistance), immediate feedback (personal empowerment), and merged awareness (Nike becomes part of the customer's internal motivation system rather than external pressure).

The Confidence Transmission Effect

Perhaps the most powerful but least understood aspect of attention capture is what we might call "confidence transmission"—the neurological process by which the marketer's genuine confidence in their message unconsciously influences audience receptiveness. Mirror neurons and emotional contagion systems mean that your internal state while creating campaigns literally transmits to audiences through subtle cues in tone, timing, word choice, and creative decisions.

High-Confidence Campaigns

- Feel inevitable rather than effortful
- Generate agreement even among those who might prefer to disagree
- Create the sense that the marketer truly believes in what they're offering
- Inspire confidence in the audience about their own judgment and choices

Low-Confidence Campaigns

- Feel desperate or manipulative despite technical competence
- Generate skepticism even when offering genuine value
- Create the sense that the marketer isn't fully convinced of their own message
- Undermine audience confidence in their decision-making

Nike's Kaepernick campaign succeeded partly because it emerged from genuine organizational conviction rather than market-tested positioning. The confidence was authentic because the risk was real—Nike genuinely believed their stance was worth potential commercial consequences.

Attention Architecture: Designing for Neural Reality

Understanding how attention actually works allows marketers to design what we might call "attention architecture"—campaign structures that naturally align with neurological attention patterns rather than fighting against them.

Pre-Attention Phase: Before conscious awareness, the brain scans for relevance signals. Effective campaigns embed these signals in headlines, imagery, opening moments, and context cues that pass initial filtering systems.

Attention Capture: Once initial filters are passed, campaigns have approximately 3-8 seconds to demonstrate value before attention moves elsewhere. This phase requires immediate value delivery or compelling curiosity activation.

Sustained Engagement: Moving from attention capture to sustained engagement requires providing continuous value, novelty, or emotional reward. The content must justify the attention investment in real-time.

Memory Encoding: For long-term impact, campaigns must activate the neurochemical systems that enhance memory formation—emotional response, personal relevance, social significance, or narrative structure.

Action Motivation: Converting attention to behavior requires aligning with existing motivation systems rather than creating new ones. The most effective calls-to-action feel like natural next steps rather than external demands.

The Social Amplification Effect

In social media environments, individual attention capture is just the beginning. The real prize is social amplification—content that not only captures attention but motivates sharing behaviors that extend reach exponentially through trusted social networks.

Neurological Sharing Triggers

- **Identity Expression:** Content that helps people signal their values, tastes, or group membership
- **Social Utility:** Information that makes the sharer look informed, caring, or connected
- **Emotional Intensity:** Experiences strong enough to motivate the effort required for sharing

- **Conversation Starters:** Content that invites response, debate, or collaboration

Nike's campaign succeeded in social amplification by providing powerful identity expression opportunities (stance-taking on social justice), social utility (sharing demonstrated awareness of important issues), emotional intensity (strong feelings regardless of political position), and conversation starting (which is impossible to encounter without having an opinion).

The Authenticity Imperative in Attention

As audiences become more sophisticated at detecting manufactured attention-seeking behaviors, authenticity becomes not just an ethical preference but a practical requirement for sustained attention capture. The brain's pattern recognition systems are remarkably good at distinguishing between genuine and performed authenticity, often below conscious awareness.

Authentic Attention Strategies

- Emerge from genuine brand values and organizational conviction
- Align marketing messages with actual company behavior and culture
- Focus on serving audience needs rather than capturing audience resources
- Accept that not everyone will be interested, rather than trying to appeal to everyone

Inauthentic Attention Strategies

- Calculate positions based purely on what will generate engagement
- Disconnect marketing messages from actual organizational reality
- Prioritize viral potential over genuine value creation
- Attempt universal appeal through focus-grouped messaging

The difference isn't always obvious to conscious analysis, but it's immediately apparent to unconscious detection systems that influence whether content feels trustworthy, interesting, or worth sharing.

Beyond Virality: Sustainable Attention Strategies

While viral campaigns capture industry attention and case study analysis, sustainable competitive advantage comes from building systematic capabilities for consistent attention capture rather than hoping for occasional breakthrough moments.

Sustainable Attention Building

- **Consistent Value Creation:** Regular content that genuinely serves audience interests
- **Authentic Voice Development:** Brand personality that reflects actual organizational culture
- **Community Engagement:** Two-way conversation rather than one-way broadcasting
- **Long-term Relationship Building:** Focus on lifetime attention rather than single-campaign breakthroughs

Unsustainable Attention Seeking

- **Manufactured Controversy:** Artificial conflict designed purely for engagement
- **Trend Chasing:** Jumping on cultural moments without an authentic connection
- **Volume Over Value:** Increased frequency without increased relevance
- **Attention Extraction:** Taking audience time without providing equivalent value

The goal isn't to create occasional viral moments but to build brands that consistently earn attention through genuine value creation and authentic connection with audience needs and interests.

The Future of Attention Competition

As artificial intelligence makes content creation increasingly accessible and social media algorithms more sophisticated, the competitive landscape for attention will continue evolving. The brands that will thrive are those that understand attention not as a resource to be captured but as a relationship to be earned.

This requires moving beyond traditional metrics of reach and impressions toward deeper measures of engagement quality, community building, and value creation. It means designing campaigns that people actively seek out rather than passively tolerate, enhancing rather than interrupting their media consumption experience.

Most importantly, it requires recognizing that in an attention economy, the scarcest resource isn't consumer attention—it's consumer gratitude. The campaigns that will define the next decade are those that leave audiences feeling genuinely served rather than successfully targeted, authentically connected rather than strategically influenced.

When marketing achieves this level of attention mastery—grounded in neurological understanding, executed with authentic confidence, and focused on genuine service—something remarkable happens: the boundary between marketing and value creation disappears. The campaign becomes indistinguishable from the value it represents, and attention flows naturally toward brands that have earned the right to receive it.

In our next chapter, we'll explore how this authentic attention capture translates into the delicate balance between optimization and authenticity that defines truly winning campaigns.

Chapter 8

Authenticity vs. Performance

The paradox of being real while optimizing for metrics—neuroscience on trust and likability

In 2013, Wendy's Twitter account was a corporate afterthought, posting generic promotional content to a modest following with minimal engagement. Then something shifted. The brand began responding to customer complaints with unexpectedly sharp wit, engaging with competitors through playful roasting, and developing a voice so distinctly irreverent that it seemed impossible it could have emerged from corporate communications guidelines.

When a user asked Wendy's how many retweets it would take for free chicken nuggets for a year, the response—"18 million"—launched what became the most retweeted post in Twitter history at the time. But the real breakthrough wasn't the viral moment; it was the emergence of a brand voice that felt simultaneously authentic and optimized, genuinely spontaneous and strategically effective.

This achievement represents one of the most challenging puzzles in modern marketing: How do you perform authentically rather than authentically perform? How do you optimize for metrics while preserving the very genuineness that makes optimization possible? How do you be strategically real without becoming really strategic?

The answer lies in understanding authenticity not as the opposite of performance, but as the highest form of it.

The Neuroscience of Authenticity Detection

Human beings possess remarkably sophisticated systems for distinguishing between authenticity and performance, most of which operate below conscious awareness. These systems evolved to help our ancestors navigate complex social environments where distinguishing between genuine cooperation and strategic manipulation was literally a matter of survival.

Micro-Expression Analysis: The brain continuously scans for micro-expressions—brief, involuntary facial expressions that reveal genuine emotional states. In marketing contexts, this translates to an unconscious assessment of whether spokesperson emotions, brand photography, and video content reflect genuine feelings rather than those that are performed.

Vocal Pattern Recognition: Beyond words themselves, the brain analyzes vocal patterns for signs of genuine versus manufactured emotion. Authentic communication exhibits subtle variations in timing, emphasis, and emotional tone that scripted communication often lacks.

Behavioral Consistency Monitoring: The brain tracks whether observed behavior aligns with stated values over time. Brands that consistently act in accordance with their communicated principles build neurological trust; those that don't trigger deep skepticism regardless of message quality.

Congruence Detection: Perhaps most importantly, the brain assesses whether different elements of communication align with each other—whether verbal, visual, and behavioral signals tell the same story or reveal internal contradiction.

Wendy's succeeded because their irreverent voice aligned consistently across contexts, their responses felt genuinely spontaneous rather than scripted, and their humor reflected actual company culture rather than adopted persona.

The Performance Paradox

The central challenge facing modern marketers is what we might call the "performance paradox": the better you get at performing authenticity, the less authentic you become. Yet some level of performance is essential for effective marketing—you can't simply be yourself without consideration for audience, context, or strategic objectives.

This paradox creates several common failure modes:

Over-Optimization: Brands that measure and adjust authenticity metrics often destroy the very quality they're trying to optimize. Authentic behavior becomes increasingly calculated and therefore increasingly inauthentic.

Meta-Awareness: When organizations become conscious of their own authenticity, they often begin performing their former genuine behavior, creating an uncanny valley effect where everything feels almost but not quite real.

Strategic Spontaneity: Attempting to plan authentic moments or spontaneous responses typically produces content that feels forced, obvious, or manufactured.

Focus Group Authenticity: Testing authentic content often reveals that what feels real to creators may not feel real to audiences, leading to modifications that improve metrics while diminishing genuine quality.

The resolution lies in understanding that authenticity isn't a trait to be maintained but a practice to be refined—a way of operating that can be systematically developed without being systematically controlled.

Performing Authentically vs. Authentically Performing

The distinction between performing authentically and authentically performing may seem semantic, but it represents a fundamental difference in approach that audiences detect unconsciously but powerfully.

Authentically Performing means

- Starting with strategic objectives and trying to appear genuine while achieving them
- Adopting personality traits or communication styles that test well but don't reflect the actual organizational culture
- Creating content designed to seem spontaneous, heartfelt, or unfiltered
- Measuring authenticity as a variable to be optimized rather than a foundation to build upon

Performing Authentically means

- Starting with genuine organizational values and finding strategic ways to express them effectively
- Developing communication approaches that amplify rather than mask the actual company personality

- Creating content that emerges from an authentic perspective while being professionally executed
- Using measurement to ensure authentic communication is reaching and serving its intended audience

The difference is subtle but neurologically detectable. Performing authentically begins with truth and uses skill to communicate it effectively. Authentically performing begins with strategy and uses simulation to make it feel true.

The Trust-Performance Integration

Neuroscientific research reveals that trust and performance aren't competing values but reinforcing systems. When audiences trust that brand communication reflects genuine values and honest intentions, they become more receptive to strategic messaging rather than less.

The Neurological Trust-Performance Loop

1. **Authentic Foundation**: Genuine organizational values and honest assessment of capabilities create internal congruence
2. **Skilled Expression**: Professional communication skills translate an authentic foundation into an effective audience connection
3. **Consistent Delivery**: Reliable alignment between promises and performance builds neurological trust patterns
4. **Enhanced Receptiveness**: Trust increases audience openness to future communication and influence
5. **Performance Amplification**: Receptive audiences respond more strongly to strategic messaging because defensive filters are reduced

This creates what we might call "earned performance"—the ability to communicate strategically because you've established that the strategy serves authentic value rather than a manipulative agenda.

Patagonia's Earned Performance: Patagonia has built such strong authenticity credentials around environmental values that its strategic marketing feels like a natural extension of its mission rather than corporate manipulation. When they tell customers "Don't buy this jacket," the message performs powerfully precisely because it reflects genuine organizational priorities.

The Likability Algorithm

Research in social psychology reveals that likability follows predictable patterns that can be understood and applied without becoming manipulative. The most likable people and brands share certain characteristics that can be systematically developed while remaining authentic to their core identity.

Neurological Likability Factors

Similarity Recognition: The brain prefers entities that seem similar to itself. Effective brands identify and amplify genuine similarities with their target audiences while remaining true to their actual identity.

Competence Demonstration: Likability requires not just warmth but also competence—the sense that the entity can deliver on its promises. This demands honest assessment and communication of actual capabilities.

Vulnerability Integration: Counter-intuitively, strategic vulnerability—acknowledging limitations or mistakes—often increases likability by demonstrating honesty and reducing threat perception.

Value Alignment: The strongest likability comes from shared values rather than shared preferences. Brands that genuinely embody values their audience cares about create a deeper connection than those that offer preferred products.

Consistent Character: Likability requires behavioral consistency over time. Audiences need to be able to predict how a brand will behave in new situations based on past behavior patterns.

The key insight is that likability can be systematically developed without being artificially manufactured, provided the development focuses on authentically expressing existing positive qualities rather than adopting foreign characteristics.

Metric-Resistant Authenticity

One of the greatest challenges in maintaining authenticity while pursuing performance is that authenticity itself resists measurement. The qualities that make communication feel genuine—spontaneity, vulnerability, emotional honesty—often decrease when they become optimization targets.

The Measurement Problem

- Authentic content often performs inconsistently, making optimization difficult
- Testing authentic communication frequently reveals what doesn't work better than what does
- Focus groups can identify inauthentic content, but struggle to create authentic alternatives
- A/B testing authentic approaches often leads to watered-down compromises that please no one

Solutions for Metric-Resistant Authenticity

Directional Rather Than Precise Measurement: Instead of optimizing specific authenticity metrics, measure whether overall brand perception is moving in authentic directions over time.

Qualitative Integration: Combine quantitative performance data with qualitative feedback about how authentic communication feels to both creators and audiences.

Cultural Consistency Tracking: Monitor whether marketing communication aligns with actual company culture and employee experience rather than just audience response.

Long-term Impact Focus: Evaluate authentic communication based on relationship building and trust development rather than immediate conversion metrics.

Internal Validation: Ensure that communication feels authentic to the people creating it, using team comfort as a key indicator of authenticity.

The Uncanny Valley of Brand Communication

Just as robotics faces the "uncanny valley"—the uncomfortable feeling produced by entities that are almost but not quite human—brand communication can fall into an authenticity uncanny valley where everything seems almost but not quite genuine.

Common Uncanny Valley Triggers

- Perfect grammar and syntax in supposedly spontaneous social media responses
- Flawless production values in content designed to seem unpolished
- Emotional expressions that are technically correct but feel slightly off
- Timing that's too convenient or responses that are too perfect
- Language that's almost but not quite how real people speak

Avoiding the Uncanny Valley

- Embrace appropriate imperfection in execution
- Allow genuine timing rather than optimal timing for responses
- Use actual employee voices rather than corporate voice, simulating employee perspectives
- Accept that authentic content won't always be optimal content
- Prioritize feeling right over testing right

Case Study: The Evolution of Corporate Social Media

The evolution of corporate social media provides a natural experiment in authenticity versus performance optimization. Early corporate accounts often felt stiff and promotional because they prioritized message control over authentic engagement. As brands learned to be more conversational, many swung toward manufactured casualness that felt equally inauthentic in a different direction.

First Generation: Strictly promotional, obviously corporate, minimal engagement

Second Generation: Attempted casualness, focus-grouped friendliness, calculated spontaneity.

Third Generation: Genuine personality expression within a professional framework

The most successful brands found ways to be genuinely themselves while being strategically effective—expressing authentic organizational personality through skilled communication rather than adopting foreign personality traits for strategic purposes.

Successful Integration Examples

- **Wendy's:** Genuinely irreverent company culture expressed through skilled social media execution
- **Mailchimp:** Authentically quirky brand personality translated into consistently charming communication
- **REI:** Genuine outdoor enthusiasm combined with professional community building
- **Buffer:** Authentic transparency about company operations merged with skilled content strategy

The Performance-Authenticity Synthesis

The highest level of marketing sophistication occurs when performance and authenticity become indistinguishable—when strategic effectiveness emerges naturally from authentic value expression rather than competing with it.

Synthesis Characteristics

- Strategic thinking enhances rather than compromises authentic expression
- Authentic values create a sustainable competitive advantage rather than limiting strategic options
- Performance metrics align with rather than contradict authenticity indicators
- Optimization improves truth-telling rather than truth-simulation
- Audience response rewards genuine value rather than manufactured appeal

Achieving Synthesis

Values-First Strategy: Begin strategic planning with an honest assessment of organizational values and build tactics that amplify rather than compromise those values.

Culture-Communication Alignment: Ensure that external communication reflects actual internal culture rather than aspirational or manufactured personality.

Authentic Advantage Identification: Identify what's genuinely distinctive about your organization and develop strategic approaches that leverage rather than hide those distinctions.

Performance Through Service: Frame performance optimization as serving audience needs more effectively rather than influencing audience behavior more successfully.

Long-term Integration: Make decisions that build authentic competitive advantage over time rather than achieving short-term performance through authenticity compromise.

The Confidence-Authenticity Connection

Perhaps the most important insight about authenticity and performance is that genuine confidence in your value proposition eliminates the perceived tension between them. When you're genuinely confident that your offering serves real customer needs, authentic communication naturally performs well because it aligns the audience's self-interest with your business objectives.

High-Confidence Authenticity

- Communicates value honestly because there's genuine value to communicate
- Accepts that not everyone will be interested, rather than trying to manufacture universal appeal
- Focuses on finding the right customers rather than convincing the wrong customers
- Uses strategic thinking to serve authenticity rather than replace it

Low-Confidence Authenticity

- Attempts to simulate confidence through performance techniques
- Tries to be appealing to everyone to compensate for an unclear value proposition
- Uses authenticity as a tactic rather than expressing it as a foundation
- Creates tension between being real and being effective

The synthesis occurs when authentic confidence in genuine value creates the foundation for strategic communication that serves both marketer and audience equally.

Beyond the False Choice

Ultimately, the opposition between authenticity and performance represents a false choice based on an incomplete understanding of both concepts. Authenticity isn't the opposite of strategy—it's the foundation for sustainable strategy. Performance isn't the enemy of genuineness—it's the skill required to communicate genuineness effectively.

The brands that will thrive in increasingly sophisticated markets are those that master what we might call "strategic authenticity"—integrating genuine values with professional communication skills, authentic personality with effective audience service, and real human connection with successful business outcomes.

This mastery doesn't come from choosing between authenticity and performance but from developing both simultaneously until they become mutually reinforcing rather than competing forces. When this integration is achieved, something remarkable happens: audiences can sense that your strategic success serves their authentic interests, creating the kind of voluntary, enthusiastic engagement that no amount of optimization alone can achieve.

In our next chapter, we'll explore how this authentic performance translates into the confidence feedback loops that create sustainable competitive advantage and genuine market leadership.

Chapter 9

The Confidence Feedback Loop

Why conviction sells better than persuasion—personal branding cases: Elon Musk, Oprah Winfrey, and niche leaders

On October 27, 2022, Elon Musk completed his acquisition of Twitter for $44 billion, despite widespread criticism that he was dramatically overpaying for a declining platform. His first act was to change his Twitter bio to "Chief Twit." His second was to carry a kitchen sink into Twitter headquarters with the caption "Entering Twitter HQ – let that sink in!" Within hours, that single tweet had generated millions of engagements, spawned countless memes, and set the tone for one of the most audacious corporate transformations in modern business history.

The sink photo wasn't sophisticated marketing. It wasn't focus-grouped, A/B tested, or strategically positioned. It was pure conviction—the neurological transmission of absolute certainty that this acquisition, this moment, this transformation was exactly what needed to happen. Whether you agreed with Musk's business judgment or not, his confidence was neurologically contagious in ways that no amount of rational argument could replicate.

This demonstrates perhaps the most powerful but least understood dynamic in marketing and personal branding: confidence doesn't just make your message more compelling—it literally changes how audiences process and respond to everything you communicate. Genuine conviction activates neurological systems that bypass skepticism, reduce resistance, and create what can only be described as influence magnetism.

The Neuroscience of Conviction Transmission

When someone speaks or acts from genuine conviction, their neurological state transmits to observers through mechanisms that operate largely below conscious awareness. Mirror neurons fire in response to authentic confidence, creating sympathetic activation of similar brain states in the audience. This isn't metaphorical influence—it's literal neurological transmission of emotional and cognitive states.

The Confidence Cascade

Internal Certainty: Genuine confidence emerges from alignment between conscious beliefs and unconscious conviction. When both systems agree that a course of action is correct, internal resistance disappears, freeing cognitive resources for execution rather than self-doubt.

Neurochemical Expression: Confidence alters posture, vocal patterns, timing, word choice, and dozens of other variables that communicate certainty below conscious perception. These micro-signals activate mirror neuron responses in observers.

Reduced Cognitive Load: Confident communication requires less mental effort to process because it doesn't trigger skepticism filters or defensive responses. Audiences can focus on content rather than assessing speaker credibility or motivation.

Social Proof Amplification: Confidence signals competence and insider knowledge, creating implicit social proof that this person knows something others don't. This activates authority and expertise response systems.

Decision-Making Facilitation: Perhaps most importantly, genuine confidence makes decision-making easier for audiences by reducing perceived risk and uncertainty around following the confident person's direction.

This neurological reality explains why conviction often succeeds where persuasion fails, and why audiences can sense authentic confidence even when they disagree with the specific message being communicated.

The Persuasion-Conviction Distinction

Traditional marketing education focuses heavily on persuasion techniques—logical arguments, emotional appeals, social proof demonstrations, and authority positioning. These approaches assume that audiences need to be convinced to act, that resistance must be overcome through superior argumentation or psychological leverage.

Conviction operates according to entirely different principles. Instead of overcoming resistance, it eliminates resistance by creating neurological certainty that reduces the perceived risk of action. Instead of providing reasons to believe, it transmits the feeling of already believing.

Persuasion Characteristics

- Argues for a position using external evidence
- Attempts to overcome objections through logical or emotional reasoning
- Works harder when encountering resistance
- Relies on technique and skill to influence outcomes
- Often creates temporary compliance rather than lasting conviction

Conviction Characteristics

- Expresses an internal certainty that feels self-evident
- Reduces objections by making alternatives seem obviously inferior
- Becomes more powerful when challenged
- Relies on authentic inner state to influence outcomes
- Creates lasting alignment rather than temporary compliance

The difference isn't just philosophical—it's neurological. Persuasion activates analytical and defensive brain systems. Conviction activates the mirror neuron and social bonding systems.

Case Study: Oprah Winfrey and Authentic Authority

Oprah Winfrey's influence empire provides perhaps the most instructive example of how authentic conviction creates sustainable competitive advantage. For over four decades, Oprah has built unparalleled audience loyalty not through sophisticated persuasion techniques but through consistent transmission of genuine conviction about human potential, spiritual growth, and authentic living.

Oprah's Confidence Architecture

Values Alignment: Oprah's public communication consistently reflects her genuine personal values rather than strategic positioning. When she recommends books, products, or ideas, audiences sense that she genuinely believes in their value rather than being paid to promote them.

Vulnerability Integration: Counter-intuitively, Oprah's willingness to share personal struggles and mistakes enhances rather than diminishes her authority. Authentic vulnerability signals confidence in one's core worth despite imperfections.

Consistent Conviction: Whether discussing weight loss, spiritual practices, social justice, or book recommendations, Oprah communicates with the same underlying conviction that people can improve their lives through conscious choice and authentic action.

Long-term Validation: Decades of consistent messaging and behavior have created cumulative credibility. Oprah's conviction feels earned rather than manufactured because it has been tested and validated over time.

Cultural Permission: Oprah has achieved the rare position where her conviction permits others to believe in possibilities they might otherwise dismiss as unrealistic or naive.

The result is an influence that transcends traditional marketing categories. When Oprah endorses a book, it becomes a bestseller not because of her reach but because of her conviction. Audiences trust that if Oprah believes a book is worth reading, it probably is—not because they've analyzed her judgment, but because her neurological certainty becomes their neurological certainty.

The Elon Musk Phenomenon: Conviction Without Consensus

Elon Musk represents a different but equally instructive example of conviction-based influence. Unlike Oprah, whose convictions align with mainstream values around personal growth and social connection, Musk's convictions often contradict conventional wisdom about business, technology, and social behavior.

Musk's Conviction Transmission

Absolute Certainty: Whether discussing Mars colonization, electric vehicle adoption, or social media transformation, Musk communicates with complete certainty that his vision represents an inevitable future reality rather than possible outcomes.

Technical Depth: Musk's conviction is supported by genuine technical expertise that allows him to speak with authority about complex subjects. This creates a rational foundation for the transmission of neurological confidence.

Indifference to Criticism: Rather than defending his positions when challenged, Musk often seems genuinely puzzled that anyone would disagree with what appears to him as an obvious truth. This indifference paradoxically strengthens conviction transmission.

Behavioral Consistency: Musk's willingness to risk personal wealth and reputation on his convictions provides neurological proof that his confidence is genuine rather than performed.

Timeline Confidence: Even when Musk's predictions prove overly optimistic, his conviction about eventual outcomes often proves correct, creating cumulative credibility for his judgment.

The result is an influence that operates independent of likability or agreement. People invest in Tesla stock, support SpaceX missions, or follow Musk's ventures not necessarily because they like him personally, but because his conviction about technological futures feels neurologically compelling.

Niche Leadership and Micro-Conviction

While Oprah and Musk represent macro-scale conviction leadership, the same principles operate at smaller scales with equally powerful results. Some of the most successful niche brands and personal brands are built on deep conviction about specific domains rather than broad appeal.

Characteristics of Successful Niche Conviction

Domain Expertise: Deep knowledge in specific areas creates an authentic foundation for conviction that generalists can't easily replicate.

Passionate Intensity: Genuine enthusiasm for specialized subjects transmits to audiences even when they don't initially share the interest.

Contrarian Confidence: Willingness to disagree with mainstream opinion when expertise suggests different conclusions creates authority through independent judgment.

Community Creation: Conviction attracts like-minded individuals who share similar values or interests, creating network effects that amplify influence.

Consistent Value Delivery: Regular demonstration of expertise through valuable content, insights, or recommendations builds cumulative credibility.

Examples of Niche Conviction Leadership

- **James Clear (habits and behavior change):** Built a massive following through a genuine conviction that small changes compound into major life improvements
- **Patrick McKenzie (software entrepreneurship):** Created an influential voice through deep conviction about business model innovation and customer value creation
- **Naval Ravikant (entrepreneurship and philosophy):** Developed a devoted following through authentic conviction about wealth creation and philosophical living
- **Brené Brown (vulnerability and courage):** Built international influence through genuine conviction about the power of authentic human connection

Each achieved influence not through broad appeal but through deep conviction in specific domains that attracted audiences seeking that particular form of certainty.

The Confidence Feedback Mechanism

Perhaps the most important aspect of conviction-based influence is its self-reinforcing nature. Genuine confidence creates results that validate the original confidence, creating upward spirals of conviction, capability, and influence.

The Feedback Loop Process

1. **Internal Conviction**: Authentic belief in value proposition or capability creates confident communication and action
2. **Audience Response**: Conviction transmission generates positive audience reaction, support, or investment
3. **Enhanced Resources**: Positive response provides increased resources (attention, capital, talent, opportunities)
4. **Improved Capability**: Additional resources enable better performance and stronger results
5. **Validated Conviction**: Strong results confirm original belief, deepening conviction for next cycle

6. **Expanded Influence**: Validated conviction attracts larger audiences and greater opportunities

This creates what economists call "increasing returns to confidence"—the more conviction you have, the more resources you attract, enabling better performance, which validates your conviction, and attracts even more resources.

Tesla's Confidence Feedback Loop

- Musk's conviction about the electric vehicle future attracts investors and talent
- Resources enable technological advancement and production scaling
- Market success validates electric vehicle thesis
- Validation deepens conviction and attracts more resources
- Increased resources enable further innovation and market expansion
- Each cycle strengthens both capability and conviction

The Dark Side of Conviction

While authentic conviction creates a powerful competitive advantage, it also carries significant risks that must be understood and managed. The same neurological systems that transmit genuine confidence can also transmit overconfidence, delusion, or misguided certainty.

Conviction Pathologies

Confirmation Bias Amplification: Strong conviction can lead to selective attention to confirming evidence while ignoring contradictory data, creating dangerous blind spots.

Resistance to Feedback: Conviction-based leaders often struggle to integrate criticism or adjust course when evidence suggests problems with their approach.

Cult-like Following: Charismatic conviction can attract followers who substitute the leader's judgment for independent thinking, creating unhealthy dependency relationships.

Reality Disconnection: In extreme cases, conviction can become disconnected from actual performance or market feedback, leading to persistent delusion despite repeated failure.

Stakeholder Exploitation: Convincing conviction can be used to extract resources from investors, customers, or employees without delivering proportional value.

The key to avoiding these pathologies is maintaining what we might call "grounded conviction"—confidence that remains connected to external reality and responsive to genuine feedback.

Building Authentic Conviction

For marketers and leaders seeking to develop authentic conviction, the challenge is building genuine confidence without falling into overconfidence or manufactured certainty. This requires systematic development of both internal conviction and external validation.

Internal Conviction Development

Values Clarification: Identify and articulate core values that feel genuinely important rather than strategically convenient. Authentic conviction emerges from alignment with deeply held beliefs.

Competence Building: Develop genuine expertise in chosen domains rather than surface-level knowledge. Real conviction requires real capability as a foundation.

Experience Integration: Process both successes and failures as learning opportunities that deepen understanding rather than random events that happen to you.

Purpose Alignment: Connect professional activities with a personal sense of meaning and contribution rather than viewing work as purely transactional.

Feedback Integration: Develop systems for receiving and processing honest feedback about performance and impact rather than surrounding yourself with agreement.

External Validation Systems

Market Testing: Regularly expose ideas and offerings to real market feedback rather than theoretical analysis alone.

Peer Review: Engage with respected experts who can provide an informed perspective on your assumptions and approaches.

Performance Tracking: Measure actual results against predictions to calibrate confidence with reality.

Stakeholder Feedback: Create channels for honest input from customers, employees, investors, and other stakeholders who have direct experience with your performance.

Continuous Learning: Maintain curiosity about new information that might challenge or refine existing convictions rather than seeking only confirming evidence.

Conviction-Based Marketing Strategies

Understanding conviction transmission provides practical guidance for creating marketing that influences through authentic confidence rather than persuasive technique.

Leadership Content: Instead of arguing for your value proposition, demonstrate conviction through consistent action and communication that assumes your value is self-evident.

Contrarian Positioning: When you genuinely disagree with conventional wisdom, express that disagreement confidently rather than hedging or over-qualifying your position.

Expertise Demonstration: Share deep knowledge and unique insights that reveal genuine expertise rather than surface-level industry commentary.

Value Assumption: Communicate as if your audience already recognizes your value rather than trying to convince them of it. This assumption often becomes self-fulfilling.

Long-term Consistency: Maintain consistent messaging and behavior over time to build cumulative credibility rather than constantly pivoting based on short-term feedback.

Authentic Vulnerability: Share appropriate struggles and uncertainties to demonstrate that your conviction exists despite rather than because of perfect conditions.

The Future of Conviction-Based Influence

As artificial intelligence makes information and analysis increasingly commoditized, and as audiences become more sophisticated at detecting manufactured persuasion, authentic conviction becomes an increasingly important competitive advantage. The leaders and brands that will thrive are those that can transmit genuine certainty about their value proposition in ways that activate rather than resist audience psychology.

This doesn't mean becoming more aggressive or dogmatic in communication, but rather becoming more authentic and grounded in genuine capability and value creation. The most influential figures of the next decade will be those who have earned the right to be confident through demonstrated competence and consistent value delivery.

When conviction is grounded in authentic capability and genuine service to audience needs, it becomes a sustainable competitive advantage that compounds over time. Audiences sense when confidence is earned rather than manufactured, and they respond to earned confidence with the kind of loyalty and engagement that no amount of sophisticated persuasion technique can replicate.

The ultimate goal isn't to become more convincing but to become more convinced—genuinely confident in your ability to serve your audience's authentic needs. When this confidence is both genuine and justified, influence flows naturally as a byproduct of competence rather than a goal to be achieved through psychological manipulation.

This completes our exploration of the psychology of winning campaigns. In Part IV, we'll examine how to integrate these insights into systematic marketing mastery that serves both commercial objectives and authentic human connection.

PART IV: MASTERY THROUGH PRACTICE

Part IV

Mastery through Practice

In Parts I through III, we've mapped the territory of marketing consciousness—from the internal dynamics that govern your creative process to the neurological realities that shape audience response, from the psychology of attention capture to the transmission of authentic conviction. We've explored how the mind creates and receives marketing messages, how stories activate empathy, how dopamine drives desire, and how confidence becomes contagious through mechanisms that operate largely outside conscious awareness.

Now we face the essential question that separates understanding from mastery: How do you integrate these insights into consistent practice? How do you move beyond knowing about the inner game of marketing to actually playing it at the highest level? How do you develop the kind of unconscious competence that allows sophisticated psychological understanding to inform your work without overwhelming your creative process?

Part IV addresses the challenge of translation—converting insights into instincts, knowledge into wisdom, and understanding into effortless execution. This isn't simply about applying techniques or following frameworks, but about developing what we might call "marketing consciousness"—a way of being and working that naturally aligns with both the psychological realities we've explored and the practical demands of creating effective campaigns in real market conditions.

The Expertise Paradox

The journey from marketing competence to marketing mastery involves a fascinating paradox that appears in all complex skill domains. As you develop a deeper understanding of the psychological and neurological principles underlying effective marketing, there's a natural tendency to become more conscious of these principles during execution. You might find yourself analyzing your creative process, evaluating your authenticity, or monitoring your audience's neurological responses, all of which can interfere with the natural flow that produces your best work.

This is the expertise paradox: the more you understand about how marketing works, the more you risk thinking your way out of the unconscious intelligence that makes marketing work. It's like a jazz musician who becomes so conscious of music theory that they can no longer improvise freely, or an athlete who becomes so aware of their technique that they lose the flow state that produces peak performance.

The resolution lies in what psychologists call "unconscious competence"—the integration of sophisticated knowledge with intuitive execution. At this level, psychological understanding doesn't compete with creative flow but enhances it, providing a foundation that supports rather than constrains natural marketing intelligence.

Master marketers don't think about mirror neurons while crafting stories, but their story construction naturally activates mirror neuron responses because they've internalized the principles that govern authentic emotional connection. They don't consciously manipulate dopamine pathways while building anticipation, but their campaign architecture naturally aligns with reward prediction systems because they understand how motivation actually works.

From Techniques to Principles

One of the most important shifts in developing marketing mastery is moving from technique-based thinking to principle-based thinking. Techniques are specific tactics that work in particular contexts—such as headline formulas, email subject line approaches, and social media engagement strategies. Principles are the underlying psychological realities that explain why techniques work and why they fail.

Technique-Based Approach

- Memorizes what has worked in specific situations
- Applies proven formulas with minor modifications

- Struggles when familiar techniques don't fit new contexts
- Relies on external authority for guidance about what to do
- Creates competent but predictable marketing

Principle-Based Approach

- Understands why certain approaches work psychologically
- Adapts underlying principles to new contexts and challenges
- Generates novel solutions when familiar approaches don't apply
- Relies on internalized understanding for guidance about what to do
- Creates sophisticated and innovative marketing

The shift from techniques to principles doesn't happen through additional study alone—it requires what we might call "applied integration," the practice of using psychological insights in real marketing contexts until they become second nature.

The Development of Marketing Intuition

Perhaps the most remarkable aspect of marketing mastery is the development of what can only be called marketing intuition—the ability to sense what will work before you can explain why, to recognize authentic connection before you can analyze its components, to know when a campaign feels right even when the data isn't yet available to confirm your assessment.

This intuition isn't mystical—it's the natural result of extensive pattern recognition combined with a deep understanding of psychological principles. When you've created hundreds of campaigns while paying attention to both the psychological dynamics and the market results, your unconscious mind develops sophisticated pattern recognition capabilities that can assess new situations faster and more accurately than conscious analysis alone.

Characteristics of Developed Marketing Intuition

- Immediate recognition of what feels authentic versus forced
- Automatic assessment of whether messaging aligns with audience psychology

- Intuitive sense of optimal timing for campaign elements
- Natural calibration of appropriate emotional intensity
- Unconscious optimization for psychological resonance

This intuition doesn't replace analytical thinking—it enhances it by providing a rapid initial assessment that can then be validated and refined through systematic analysis. The most effective marketers learn to trust their intuitive guidance while remaining open to information that might contradict their initial sense.

The Practice of Conscious Competence

Developing marketing mastery requires what we might call "conscious practice"—deliberately applying psychological insights in real marketing contexts while paying attention to both the internal experience of creation and the external results of execution. This is different from both unconscious practice (doing marketing without awareness of underlying principles) and purely analytical study (understanding principles without applying them in practice).

Elements of Conscious Practice

Intentional Application: Deliberately practicing specific psychological principles in real marketing contexts rather than waiting for perfect conditions or complete understanding.

Process Awareness: Paying attention to your internal experience while creating campaigns—noticing when you're flowing versus forcing, when you feel confident versus uncertain, when approaches feel authentic versus manufactured.

Outcome Integration: Connecting campaign results with the psychological principles and internal processes that produced them, building understanding of what works when and why.

Feedback Responsiveness: Using market response, audience feedback, and business results to refine your understanding of how psychological principles apply in your specific context.

Iterative Refinement: Treating each campaign as an experiment that contributes to your developing mastery rather than a standalone success or failure.

The Integration Challenge

Perhaps the greatest challenge in developing marketing mastery is learning to integrate multiple forms of intelligence simultaneously. Effective marketing requires analytical thinking, creative insight, emotional intelligence, social awareness, and business acumen—often all at the same time. The challenge isn't developing each capability independently but learning to access and integrate them fluidly depending on what each situation requires.

The Integration Requirements

Analytical-Creative Integration: Using logical thinking to support rather than constrain creative insight, finding the sweet spot where strategic rigor enhances rather than diminishes imaginative possibility.

Internal-External Balance: Maintaining authentic self-expression while remaining genuinely responsive to audience needs and market dynamics, avoiding both self-indulgent creativity and soulless optimization.

Confidence-Humility Synthesis: Communicating with conviction while remaining open to feedback and course correction, projecting authority while maintaining curiosity about what you might not yet understand.

Service-Success Alignment: Pursuing business objectives through genuine value creation rather than despite it, finding approaches that serve both commercial goals and authentic human needs.

Present-Future Orientation: Remaining fully present to current creative and strategic demands while maintaining awareness of long-term brand building and relationship development.

This integration can't be achieved through willpower or technique alone—it requires the kind of systematic practice that allows these capabilities to develop naturally and work together harmoniously.

The Path from Competence to Artistry

The ultimate goal of marketing mastery isn't just professional competence but what we might call "marketing artistry"—the ability to create campaigns that transcend purely commercial objectives to become genuine contributions to culture, consciousness, and human connection. This level of work serves business objectives precisely because it authentically meets human needs, making commercial success a natural byproduct of genuine value creation.

Characteristics of Marketing Artistry

- Creates campaigns that feel inevitable in retrospect but surprising in the moment
- Generates work that audiences actively seek out rather than passively tolerate
- Builds brands that customers feel genuinely grateful to have discovered
- Produces marketing that enhances rather than pollutes the cultural environment
- Achieves commercial success through rather than despite authentic service

This artistry emerges not from additional techniques but from the complete integration of psychological understanding with authentic personal expression and genuine commitment to serving audience needs. It represents marketing that has transcended the traditional categories of art versus commerce, authenticity versus effectiveness, and creativity versus strategy.

The Lifelong Practice

Perhaps the most important insight about marketing mastery is that it represents a lifelong practice rather than a destination to be reached. Human psychology continues evolving, market conditions continue changing, and your own understanding continues deepening throughout your career. The goal isn't to achieve perfect marketing capability but to develop the kind of conscious competence that allows you to continue learning and growing while consistently creating valuable work.

Characteristics of Lifelong Practice

- Maintains beginner's mind despite accumulated expertise
- Views each campaign as an opportunity for learning rather than just a business objective
- Seeks feedback from multiple sources, including audiences, peers, and results
- Experiments with new approaches while maintaining proven capabilities
- Integrates insights from psychology, neuroscience, culture, and business as they emerge

This practice orientation transforms marketing from a job you do into a craft you develop, from a set of skills you possess into a way of consciousness you cultivate. It makes the work itself intrinsically rewarding while also producing the kind of external results that create sustainable competitive advantage.

The Service Integration

The highest level of marketing mastery occurs when serving your audience's authentic needs becomes indistinguishable from serving your business objectives. At this level, the traditional tension between commercial success and genuine service disappears because you've learned to create value so authentically that customers actively want to support your business success.

This integration requires moving beyond thinking about marketing as something you do to customers toward thinking about it as something you do with customers—collaborative value creation where your marketing helps customers achieve their goals while achieving your own. When this collaboration is genuine, influence becomes mutual rather than unidirectional, and success becomes shared rather than extracted.

The Invitation to Mastery

Part IV explores how to develop this level of marketing consciousness through three essential dimensions: understanding the internal dialogue between analytical and creative thinking, learning to listen to market feedback in ways that enhance rather than compromise authentic expression, and developing the resilience and adaptability that allow you to maintain both effectiveness and integrity throughout the inevitable challenges of professional growth.

This isn't about becoming a different kind of marketer—it's about becoming more fully the marketer you already are, freed from the internal interference and external pressures that prevent your natural marketing intelligence from expressing itself most effectively. The principles we've explored throughout this book provide the foundation. Still, mastery emerges through the conscious practice of applying them in real contexts with genuine commitment to serving both your authentic creative vision and your audience's legitimate needs.

Welcome to the path of marketing mastery, where understanding becomes wisdom, techniques become principles, and competence becomes artistry in the service of both commercial success and authentic human connection.

Chapter 10

Self 1 vs. Self 2 in the Marketer's Journey

Inner dialogue: analyst vs creator—from campaign paralysis to intuitive execution

Anika stared at the blank presentation slide, cursor blinking accusingly in the title field. Three weeks into developing the campaign strategy for her company's most important product launch, she found herself trapped in an internal debate that had become devastatingly familiar.

Self 1 (the voice of analysis and control): "The market research clearly indicates that emotional messaging performs 23% better than rational appeals in this demographic, but the competitive analysis suggests that differentiation through feature emphasis might be more defensible long-term. We should probably run additional focus groups to validate the positioning before committing to a creative direction."

Self 2 (the voice of natural marketing intelligence): "This product helps working parents feel more confident about their family's financial future. The campaign should feel like a trusted friend who understands their fears and genuinely believes this solution will help. Everything else is secondary."

The tension between these two voices—one demanding more analysis, the other urging authentic action—had paralyzed Anika's creative process for weeks. Every insight from Self 2 was immediately questioned by Self 1. Every strategic framework proposed by Self 1 felt hollow to Self 2. What should have been her most important campaign was becoming her most frustrating professional experience.

This internal conflict represents one of the most common and least addressed challenges in marketing development: the ongoing dialogue between what Tim Gallwey called Self 1 (the conscious, analytical, controlling voice) and Self 2 (the unconscious, intuitive, naturally competent voice). Understanding this dialogue—and learning to orchestrate it productively—may be the most important skill for developing marketing mastery.

The Anatomy of Internal Marketing Dialogue

Every marketer carries on continuous internal conversations that shape both the creative process and the final output. These conversations typically involve multiple voices, but two are particularly important for marketing effectiveness:

Self 1: The Internal Analyst. This is the voice of conscious thinking, strategic frameworks, market research, and optimization. Self 1 wants to get everything right, avoid mistakes, and create work that can be logically defended. It speaks in metrics, methodologies, and best practices. It's the voice that says, "We need more data," or "this approach hasn't been validated," or "what if this doesn't work?"

Self 2: The Natural Marketing Intelligence. This is the voice of intuitive understanding, creative insight, and natural human connection. Self 2 knows how to communicate authentically, recognizes what feels genuine versus forced, and trusts that audiences respond to sincerity more than sophistication. It speaks in feelings, stories, and immediate recognition. It's the voice that says, "This feels right," or "our audience will connect with this," or "trust the process."

Neither voice is wrong, but their relationship determines whether marketing development feels effortless or agonizing, whether campaigns feel authentic or calculated, and whether results emerge from genuine connection or strategic manipulation.

The Evolution of Internal Dialogue

The relationship between Self 1 and Self 2 evolves throughout a marketer's career in predictable patterns that mirror skill development in other complex domains. Understanding these patterns can help you navigate the inevitable tensions while accelerating your development toward mastery.

Stage 1: Unconscious Incompetence (Beginner)

- Self 2 operates freely but lacks knowledge and skill
- Self 1 hasn't yet developed sophisticated analytical capabilities
- Natural enthusiasm compensates for limited expertise

- Mistakes happen frequently, but learning occurs rapidly
- Creative output feels authentic but may lack strategic sophistication

Example: A new marketer creates an email campaign based purely on gut feeling about what their audience wants to hear. The message feels genuine but completely ignores deliverability best practices, leading to poor performance despite strong emotional resonance.

Stage 2: Conscious Incompetence (Developing Professional)

- Self 1 begins developing analytical frameworks and strategic knowledge
- Self 2's instincts get questioned and often overridden
- Internal conflict emerges as analytical thinking competes with intuitive insights
- Campaign development becomes more effortful and less enjoyable
- Work becomes more technically competent, but may lose authentic feeling

Example: The same marketer, now equipped with A/B testing knowledge and demographic data, spends weeks optimizing email subject lines but creates campaigns that feel focus-grouped and sterile despite better open rates.

Stage 3: Conscious Competence (Experienced Professional)

- Self 1 has developed sophisticated analytical capabilities
- Self 2 continues operating but often gets suppressed in favor of "proven" approaches
- Marketing becomes technically proficient but may feel mechanical
- Success comes through skill and knowledge rather than natural connection
- Internal dialogue becomes more collaborative, but Self 1 typically dominates

Example: Now a senior marketer, they can execute complex multi-channel campaigns with strong performance metrics, but colleagues notice their work lacks the creative spark it once had.

Stage 4: Unconscious Competence (Marketing Mastery)

- Self 1 and Self 2 work in harmony rather than in competition
- Analytical thinking supports rather than constrains intuitive insights
- Technical competence serves authentic communication rather than replacing it
- Campaign development feels both effortless and sophisticated
- Internal dialogue becomes a collaborative resource rather than an internal conflict

Example: The same marketer now trusts their intuitive sense of what will resonate while using analytical skills to execute and optimize that intuition effectively. Campaigns feel both strategically sound and authentically engaging.

The Paralysis Pattern

The most destructive pattern in internal marketing dialogue occurs when Self 1 becomes so dominant that it paralyzes Self 2's natural competence. This typically happens when marketers become afraid of making mistakes, over-rely on data to avoid creative risk, or lose confidence in their natural ability to connect with audiences.

Common Paralysis Triggers

Analysis Addiction: Using additional research, testing, or strategic planning as a way to avoid the vulnerability inherent in authentic creative expression.

Perfectionism Spiral: Setting impossible standards that prevent any campaign from feeling ready for launch, often disguised as "professional rigor."

Comparison Trap: Constantly measuring creative work against industry benchmarks or competitor campaigns rather than trusting the authentic voice and approach.

Metric Fixation: Optimizing for measurable outcomes while losing sight of immeasurable but essential qualities like authenticity, emotional resonance, or genuine service.

External Validation Dependency: Requiring approval from multiple stakeholders or focus groups before trusting that a campaign direction feels right.

When these patterns dominate, marketing development becomes increasingly effortful while producing increasingly sterile results. The work may test well and perform adequately, but it lacks the indefinable quality that creates genuine connection and lasting impact.

The Integration Path

The goal isn't to choose between analytical thinking and intuitive insight, but to develop what we might call "conscious collaboration" between Self 1 and Self 2. This requires understanding when each voice is most valuable and learning to orchestrate their contributions rather than letting them compete.

Self 2 Leadership Situations

- Initial creative concept development
- Authenticity assessment ("Does this feel real?")
- Emotional tone and voice decisions
- Story and narrative construction
- Breakthrough insight generation
- Cultural and social sensitivity evaluation

Self 1 Leadership Situations

- Strategic framework development
- Technical execution planning
- Performance measurement and optimization
- Risk assessment and mitigation
- Resource allocation and timeline management
- Legal and compliance considerations

Collaborative Integration Situations

- Campaign positioning that's both strategically sound and emotionally resonant
- Creative execution that serves business objectives through authentic value creation

- Message testing that validates intuitive insights without destroying their authenticity
- Performance analysis that informs future intuitive decision-making
- Stakeholder communication that builds confidence in creative direction

Practical Integration Techniques

Developing productive internal dialogue requires specific practices that honor both analytical rigor and creative authenticity. These techniques help orchestrate Self 1 and Self 2 collaboration rather than leaving their relationship to chance.

The Two-Phase Approach: Begin campaign development with dedicated Self 2 time—creative exploration without immediate analytical evaluation. Generate concepts, explore directions, and trust initial instincts without premature optimization. Then bring Self 1 online to evaluate, refine, and execute the most promising directions.

The Internal Advisor Model: Treat Self 1 as a skilled advisor to Self 2 rather than a replacement for it. Use analytical thinking to support creative insight ("How can we execute this intuitive direction most effectively?") rather than to generate creative direction ("What does the data suggest we should create?").

The Authenticity Check: Before finalizing any campaign element, ask Self 2: "Does this feel genuine?" If the answer is no, use Self 1 to identify what specifically feels inauthentic and explore modifications that preserve both strategic effectiveness and emotional truth.

The Strategic Foundation: Use Self 1 to establish clear strategic parameters (audience, objectives, constraints) that provide a framework within which Self 2 can operate freely. Clear boundaries often enhance rather than limit creative freedom.

The Iterative Dialogue: Create structured conversations between Self 1 and Self 2 throughout campaign development. After each creative decision, ask: "What does analysis suggest about this direction?" After each analytical insight, ask: "How does this feel from an authenticity perspective?"

Case Study: From Paralysis to Flow

Consider the transformation of Marcus, a marketing director who had become trapped in analysis paralysis after several campaign failures early in his tenure.

His Self 1 had become hypervigilant, demanding extensive validation for every creative choice, while his Self 2 had essentially gone silent under the pressure.

The Paralysis Phase

- Campaign development took 3-4 months due to endless research and testing cycles
- Creative concepts felt safe but uninspiring
- Performance was adequate but lacked breakthrough potential
- Personal satisfaction with work diminished despite professional competence
- Team dynamics suffered as perfectionism created unrealistic timelines

The Integration Process: Marcus worked with a coach to identify when his analytical voice was serving versus constraining his creative process. He began experimenting with structured creative sessions where analytical evaluation was deliberately delayed, allowing natural marketing intelligence to operate freely before bringing strategic thinking online.

The Flow Phase

- Campaign development accelerated to 4-6 weeks while improving quality
- Creative concepts felt both authentic and strategically sound
- Performance improved as an authentic connection enhanced analytical optimization
- Personal satisfaction returned as work felt meaningful rather than just competent
- Team dynamics improved as a clear, creative vision reduced internal debate

The key insight wasn't abandoning analytical thinking but learning when and how to apply it most effectively to support, rather than replace, natural marketing intelligence.

The Confidence Component

Perhaps the most important factor in productive Self 1/Self 2 dialogue is the underlying confidence level in your natural marketing abilities. When you trust that Self 2 has genuine wisdom about human connection and authentic communication, Self 1 can serve as a supportive advisor. When you doubt Self 2's competence, Self 1 becomes a controlling supervisor that undermines natural intelligence.

High-Confidence Integration

- Self 1 asks: "How can we execute this insight most effectively?"
- Self 2 trusts: "This direction feels right, let's figure out implementation."
- Collaboration: "Our intuition plus strategic thinking creates powerful campaigns."

Low-Confidence Domination

- Self 1 asks: "What does the data tell us we should do?"
- Self 2 doubts: "Maybe my instincts are wrong, better trust the research"
- Competition: "We need to choose between being strategic or authentic."

Building confidence in Self 2 requires paying attention to when intuitive insights prove accurate, celebrating campaigns that succeed through authentic connection, and recognizing that natural marketing intelligence can be trusted and developed rather than replaced by analytical thinking.

The Cultural Context

The balance between Self 1 and Self 2 is significantly influenced by organizational culture and industry norms. Some environments heavily reward analytical thinking while viewing intuitive insights as unprofessional or risky. Others celebrate creativity while dismissing strategic rigor as limiting or soulless.

Analytical-Dominant Cultures

- Require extensive justification for creative decisions
- Prefer incremental optimization over breakthrough innovation
- May inadvertently suppress Self 2 through over-emphasis on measurement
- Often produces competent but unremarkable marketing

Creative-Dominant Cultures

- May dismiss strategic planning as limiting creative potential
- Can produce innovative but commercially ineffective campaigns
- Sometimes ignore market realities in favor of artistic expression
- Often struggle with consistent performance measurement

Integrated Cultures

- Value both strategic thinking and creative insight
- Create space for intuitive exploration within strategic frameworks
- Measure both analytical performance and authentic connection
- Produce marketing that's both commercially successful and culturally influential

Understanding your cultural context helps you navigate the Self 1/Self 2 dialogue in ways that serve both your authentic creative development and your professional success within existing organizational realities.

The Mastery Perspective

At the highest levels of marketing mastery, the distinction between Self 1 and Self 2 becomes less relevant because both functions become integrated into unified marketing consciousness. Master marketers don't think about whether to trust analysis or intuition—they fluidly access whichever form of intelligence the situation requires while maintaining awareness of both.

Characteristics of Integrated Marketing Consciousness

- Automatic calibration between analytical and intuitive thinking
- Strategic frameworks that enhance rather than constrain creative freedom
- Intuitive insights that naturally align with business objectives
- Campaign development that feels both effortless and sophisticated
- Results that satisfy both analytical metrics and authentic service goals

This integration doesn't eliminate internal dialogue but transforms it from competition into collaboration. The voices become resources to be orchestrated rather than opponents to be chosen between.

Beyond the Internal Conversation

Ultimately, the most important insight about Self 1 versus Self 2 is that productive internal dialogue serves something larger than either voice alone: the genuine service of your audience's authentic needs. When both analytical thinking and intuitive insight are oriented toward creating real value for real people, they naturally support rather than compete with each other.

The internal conversation becomes less about whether to trust your head or your heart and more about how to integrate both in service of work that truly matters. This service orientation resolves many internal conflicts because it provides a shared purpose that both Self 1 and Self 2 can support.

In our next chapter, we'll explore how this internal integration translates into enhanced ability to listen to and learn from market feedback in ways that deepen rather than compromise your authentic marketing voice.

Chapter 11

The Art of Listening to the Market

Active listening as neural mirroring—how Patagonia built a brand from listening

In 1973, Yvon Chouinard was facing a crisis that would define both his company and the future of conscious capitalism. His fledgling business, Patagonia, had built its reputation creating climbing equipment. Still, Chouinard was discovering that his signature product—reusable pitons for rock climbing—was actually damaging the very rock formations that climbers cherished. The feedback wasn't coming through focus groups or market research surveys. It was coming through direct observation of scarred cliff faces and passionate conversations with fellow climbers who loved the gear but hated what it was doing to their playground.

Most business leaders would have dismissed this feedback as irrelevant to commercial success. The pitons were profitable, popular, and had no obvious substitute. Customer satisfaction scores were high. But Chouinard possessed a rare ability to listen not just to what customers were saying explicitly, but to what the market ecosystem was expressing implicitly about the long-term consequences of his business choices.

He made the radical decision to abandon his most profitable product line and develop removable climbing protection instead—gear that would preserve the rock while serving climbers' safety needs. This decision emerged not from market analysis but from what we might call "systemic listening"—attention to the complex web of relationships, values, and consequences that surround any business decision.

That ability to listen deeply to market signals that go beyond immediate customer feedback has become Patagonia's defining competitive advantage, enabling it to anticipate cultural shifts, build extraordinary customer loyalty, and create a brand that customers don't just buy from but actively advocate for.

The Neuroscience of Market Listening

Understanding how to listen effectively to market feedback requires examining what actually happens neurologically when we encounter information that might contradict our existing beliefs, challenge our strategic assumptions, or suggest uncomfortable truths about our work.

The human brain is equipped with sophisticated filtering systems designed to maintain cognitive consistency and protect existing worldviews. When information conflicts with our established beliefs, several neurological defense mechanisms activate automatically:

Confirmation Bias Amplification: The brain preferentially notices and remembers information that confirms existing beliefs while minimizing attention to contradictory evidence. For marketers, this means unconsciously seeking feedback that validates current approaches while dismissing signals that suggest different directions.

Cognitive Dissonance Resolution: When confronted with information that contradicts established views, the brain experiences uncomfortable tension and automatically seeks ways to reduce this dissonance—often by discrediting the source, reinterpreting the information, or finding reasons why it doesn't apply to current circumstances.

Identity Protection Systems: Feedback that suggests our professional competence, creative judgment, or strategic thinking might be flawed triggers defensive responses designed to protect self-concept rather than integrate new information.

Social Conformity Pressure: The brain's social detection systems make us particularly sensitive to feedback that might isolate us from professional peers or challenge industry conventional wisdom.

These neurological realities mean that effective market listening isn't just about collecting more feedback—it requires developing the psychological capacity to remain open to information that might be uncomfortable, inconvenient, or challenging to integrate.

The Difference between Hearing and Listening

Most marketing feedback systems are designed for hearing rather than listening. They collect quantitative data, track behavioral metrics, and gather explicit customer opinions. Still, they often miss the deeper patterns, implicit tensions, and emerging shifts that represent the most valuable market intelligence.

Hearing Market Signals

- Focuses on explicit, measurable feedback
- Seeks information that can be easily categorized and analyzed
- Prioritizes volume and statistical significance
- Often confirms existing assumptions rather than challenging them
- Operates through predetermined questions and frameworks

Listening to Market Wisdom

- Attends to implicit patterns and emerging themes
- Remains open to information that doesn't fit existing categories
- Values depth and nuance over volume and certainty
- Actively seeks disconfirming evidence and alternative perspectives
- Allows new frameworks to emerge from observed patterns

The difference isn't just methodological—it's neurological. Hearing operates primarily through System 1 pattern recognition, quickly categorizing new information according to existing frameworks. Listening requires engaging System 2 analytical thinking while maintaining System 1 openness to novel patterns that might not fit predetermined categories.

The Mirror Neuron Effect in Market Research

One of the most important but least recognized aspects of market listening involves what neuroscientists call "neural mirroring"—the unconscious synchronization of brain states between observer and observed. When you're truly listening to customer feedback, your mirror neurons activate in response to the emotional and psychological states of the people providing that feedback.

This creates a form of embodied market research that goes far beyond verbal or written responses. When customers are frustrated, confused, excited, or skeptical, skilled listeners can detect these states not just through explicit statements but also through subtle changes in vocal tone, body language, timing, and energy, which activate corresponding states in the listener's nervous system.

Practical Applications of Neural Mirroring

Customer Interview Depth: Instead of focusing only on what customers say, pay attention to how they feel while saying it. Energy shifts, hesitations, and enthusiasm often reveal more about genuine preferences than carefully considered verbal responses.

Social Media Sentiment: Beyond analyzing positive and negative keywords, notice the emotional energy in customer communications. Authentic excitement feels different from polite satisfaction; genuine frustration feels different from performative complaint.

Community Dynamics: Observe not just individual feedback but the collective emotional patterns in customer communities. Shifts in overall energy, engagement levels, and conversation topics often predict market changes before they show up in traditional metrics.

Cultural Undercurrents: Pay attention to broader cultural and social patterns that your customers are embedded within. Their responses to your brand are influenced by much larger contexts that rarely appear in direct feedback.

Patagonia's Systemic Listening Approach

Patagonia's success in building both commercial value and cultural influence stems largely from its sophisticated approach to market listening that goes far beyond traditional customer feedback. They've developed what might be called "ecosystem listening"—attention to the complex web of relationships, values, and consequences that surround their business.

Multi-Level Listening Framework

Customer Voice: Direct feedback from people who buy and use Patagonia products, gathered through traditional and innovative channels.

Community Wisdom: Insights from the broader outdoor recreation community, including non-customers who share similar values and face similar challenges.

Environmental Feedback: Information from the natural ecosystems that outdoor enthusiasts depend on, treated as a stakeholder whose "voice" is expressed through environmental data and ecological health indicators.

Cultural Signals: Attention to broader social movements, generational shifts, and evolving values that influence how people think about consumption, corporate responsibility, and authentic living.

Supply Chain Intelligence: Feedback from manufacturing partners, suppliers, and workers throughout their global production network about both operational realities and social impacts.

Future Orientation: Systematic consideration of how current business decisions will affect long-term relationships with all stakeholders, even when short-term impacts might be positive.

This multi-dimensional listening approach allows Patagonia to anticipate market shifts, identify authentic value creation opportunities, and make decisions that strengthen rather than compromise their core relationships over time.

The Paradox of Listening for Authenticity

One of the most challenging aspects of market listening for authenticity-focused brands is that asking directly about authenticity often destroys the very quality you're trying to measure. When customers are explicitly asked whether something feels "authentic" or "genuine," they often provide responses based on their analytical assessment rather than their immediate felt experience.

The Authenticity Measurement Problem

- Direct questions about authenticity trigger analytical rather than intuitive responses
- Focus group environments often suppress authentic reactions in favor of socially acceptable responses
- A/B testing authentic content frequently leads to optimization that diminishes authenticity
- Survey instruments struggle to capture the subtle qualities that make communication feel genuine

Alternative Listening Approaches

Behavioral Observation: Watch what customers do rather than relying only on what they say. Authentic connection often manifests in engagement patterns, sharing behaviors, and voluntary advocacy rather than explicit feedback.

Emotional Mapping: Pay attention to the emotional journey customers experience with your brand over time. Authentic relationships typically deepen and become more personally meaningful rather than remaining transactional.

Spontaneous Expression: Notice unsolicited feedback, voluntary testimonials, and organic social media mentions that customers create without prompting. These often reveal authentic responses better than requested feedback.

Community Evolution: Observe how customer communities develop their own language, rituals, and relationships around your brand. Authentic brands often catalyze genuine community formation rather than manufactured engagement.

Long-term Relationship Patterns: Track how customer relationships with your brand evolve over months and years rather than focusing only on immediate responses to specific campaigns.

Active Listening Techniques for Marketers

Developing sophisticated market listening capabilities requires specific techniques that go beyond traditional research methodologies. These approaches help marketers access the deeper intelligence that emerges when you create genuine space for market wisdom to express itself.

The Beginner's Mind Interview: Approach customer conversations with genuine curiosity about their experience rather than predetermined hypotheses to validate. Ask open-ended questions that invite storytelling rather than category-based responses: "Tell me about a time when..." rather than "Rate your satisfaction with..."

The Silent Space Technique: Create comfortable silence in conversations that allows deeper thoughts and feelings to emerge. Many of the most valuable insights come not from immediate responses but from the reflections that follow when people have time to process their actual experiences.

The Contrarian Question Method: Actively seek information that challenges your assumptions by asking questions designed to surface problems, limitations, or alternative perspectives: "What would need to change for you to stop using our product?" or "Who do you think we serve poorly?"

The Cultural Context Exploration: Understand customer feedback within broader life contexts rather than just product experiences. How does your offering fit into their relationships, values, aspirations, and challenges that have nothing to do with your specific category?

The Emotional Archaeology Approach: Look for the feelings underneath explicit statements. When someone says "it's fine" or "it works okay," explore what emotional experience that represents. Neutral language often masks either deep satisfaction or significant disappointment.

Integrating Quantitative and Qualitative Intelligence

The most sophisticated market listening combines quantitative behavioral data with qualitative emotional and cultural intelligence. Neither alone provides a complete understanding, but together they can reveal patterns that transform strategic thinking.

Quantitative Intelligence Strengths

- Reveals what customers do at scale
- Identifies statistically significant patterns
- Tracks changes over time with precision
- Enables prediction based on historical patterns
- Provides an objective foundation for decision-making

Qualitative Intelligence Strengths

- Reveals why customers behave as they do
- Identifies emerging patterns before they become statistically significant
- Captures emotional and cultural nuances that influence behavior
- Enables understanding of context and meaning
- Provides subjective insight that informs strategic intuition

Integration Approaches

Data-Story Integration: Use quantitative data to identify interesting patterns, then use qualitative exploration to understand the human stories behind those patterns.

Hypothesis Generation: Use qualitative insights to develop hypotheses about market dynamics, then use quantitative analysis to validate or refine those hypotheses.

Anomaly Investigation: When quantitative data shows unexpected results, use qualitative investigation to understand what cultural or emotional shifts might be driving those changes.

Predictive Triangulation: Combine quantitative trend analysis with qualitative cultural observation to predict future market shifts before they appear in mainstream data.

The Feedback Integration Challenge

Perhaps the most difficult aspect of sophisticated market listening is learning to integrate challenging feedback without losing authentic voice or compromising genuine value creation. The goal isn't to become what customers explicitly ask for, but to understand their deeper needs well enough to serve them in ways they might not have imagined.

Productive Feedback Integration

- Maintains core brand values while adapting execution approaches
- Uses customer insights to improve authentic value creation rather than replacing it
- Distinguishes between feedback about execution versus feedback about fundamental direction
- Builds a stronger rather than broader appeal through a deeper understanding of core audience needs

Destructive Feedback Integration

- Abandons authentic differentiation in favor of generic appeal
- Uses customer requests to drive brand strategy rather than inform tactical decisions
- Attempts to satisfy every customer segment rather than serving the core audience exceptionally well
- Prioritizes immediate approval over long-term relationship building

The key is developing what we might call "discerning responsiveness"—the ability to hear and integrate valuable feedback while maintaining the authentic foundation that makes your brand worth listening to in the first place.

Building Listening Capabilities Organizationally

Individual listening skills are important, but sustainable competitive advantage comes from building organizational capabilities for sophisticated market intelligence that go beyond any single person's abilities.

Organizational Listening Infrastructure

Distributed Sensing: Create systems where multiple people throughout the organization regularly interact with customers and provide insights to central intelligence, rather than limiting market contact to designated research roles.

Cultural Listening Competence: Develop widespread capability to distinguish between surface feedback and deeper market intelligence rather than concentrating listening skills in specialized roles.

Cross-Functional Integration: Ensure that insights from customer service, sales, product development, and marketing combine to create a comprehensive market understanding rather than remaining in departmental silos.

Long-term Pattern Recognition: Build institutional memory that tracks market evolution over years rather than focusing only on immediate feedback cycles.

Experimental Learning Culture: Foster organizational comfort by testing new approaches based on market signals, rather than requiring extensive validation before responding to emerging insights.

The Future of Market Listening

As artificial intelligence makes data collection and analysis increasingly sophisticated, the competitive advantage in market listening will shift toward the uniquely human capabilities that technology cannot replicate: emotional intelligence, cultural intuition, systemic thinking, and the ability to integrate complex, contradictory information into coherent strategic insight.

The brands that will thrive are those that develop what we might call "conscious listening"—market intelligence gathering that honors both analytical rigor and intuitive wisdom, that serves both commercial objectives and authentic value creation, that builds both competitive advantage and genuine stakeholder relationships.

This requires moving beyond viewing market listening as information extraction and instead considering it as relationship building—ongoing dialogue with all stakeholders that fosters mutual understanding and shared value creation rather than just competitive advantage.

The Service of Deep Listening

At its highest level, market listening becomes a form of service—genuine attention to stakeholder needs, concerns, and aspirations that goes beyond commercial utility to encompass authentic care for the people and communities your business affects. When listening is motivated by genuine service rather than just strategic advantage, it often reveals opportunities for value creation that serve both business objectives and stakeholder wellbeing.

This service orientation doesn't diminish commercial effectiveness—it enhances it by creating the kind of authentic relationships that generate sustainable competitive advantage. When customers, communities, and other stakeholders feel genuinely heard and understood, they respond with the kind of loyalty and advocacy that no amount of traditional marketing can create.

In our next chapter, we'll explore how this deep listening capability, combined with authentic value creation, builds the resilience and adaptability needed to sustain marketing excellence through the inevitable challenges of professional and market evolution.

Chapter 12

Resilience and Adaptability

Handling failure like experiments, not verdicts—case study: Netflix pivoting from DVDs to streaming

On September 18, 2011, Reed Hastings published a blog post that temporarily destroyed Netflix's stock price, triggered massive customer cancellations, and became one of the most criticized corporate communications in business history. In 900 words titled "An Explanation and Some Reflections," Hastings apologized for poor communication around price increases and announced that Netflix would split its DVD and streaming services into separate companies, with the DVD business rebranded as "Qwikster."

The market response was brutal. Netflix stock dropped 35% in the following weeks. Over 800,000 customers canceled their subscriptions. Late-night comedians mocked the company relentlessly. Industry analysts declared that Netflix had committed strategic suicide. The consensus was clear: Hastings had made a catastrophic error that would permanently damage the company's position in the entertainment industry.

But something remarkable happened in Hastings' response to this failure. Instead of defending the decision, minimizing the damage, or blaming external factors, he demonstrated what might be called "experimental resilience"—the ability to treat even spectacular failures as valuable information rather than identity-threatening verdicts. Within weeks, Netflix abandoned the Qwikster plan, explicitly acknowledged the mistakes, and used market feedback to accelerate its transition to streaming while maintaining its DVD business under the original brand.

More importantly, Hastings and his team used this painful experience to deepen their understanding of customer psychology, communication strategy, and market timing. The lessons learned from this failure directly informed the strategic thinking that would eventually make Netflix the dominant force in streaming entertainment, with a market capitalization that would grow from $4 billion in 2011 to over $240 billion by 2021.

This case illustrates perhaps the most crucial capability for sustained marketing excellence: the ability to maintain both effectiveness and authenticity through inevitable failures, market shifts, and professional challenges that would derail less resilient practitioners.

The Neuroscience of Resilient Learning

Understanding how to bounce back from marketing failures requires examining what happens neurologically when unexpected results, harsh feedback, or spectacular mistakes challenge our professional competence. The brain's response to perceived threats—including threats to professional identity—can either enhance or completely undermine our ability to learn from difficult experiences.

Threat Response Patterns

When failure activates the brain's threat detection systems, several neurological responses typically occur:

Amygdala Activation: The brain's alarm system triggers fight-or-flight responses that prioritize immediate survival over learning and adaptation. This makes it difficult to process complex information or consider multiple perspectives when dealing with failure.

Cortisol Release: Stress hormones flood the system, impairing memory formation, reducing cognitive flexibility, and creating a psychological state focused on threat elimination rather than opportunity identification.

Ego Defense Mechanisms: The brain automatically generates explanations that protect the self-concept rather than accurately assess what happened. This leads to blame attribution, rationalization, and other responses that feel protective but prevent genuine learning.

Cognitive Tunnel Vision: Under stress, attention narrows to immediate threats, making it difficult to see broader patterns, long-term implications, or alternative interpretations that might reveal valuable insights.

Resilient Learning Patterns

However, individuals who consistently learn and improve from failures show different neurological patterns:

Prefrontal Cortex Engagement: The brain's executive functions remain online during failure processing, enabling analytical thinking, perspective-taking, and strategic planning rather than pure emotional reaction.

Growth Mindset Activation: Failure activates neural networks associated with learning and development, rather than just threat and protection, fostering curiosity about improvement instead of concern about damage.

Pattern Recognition Enhancement: Instead of defensive responses, failure triggers enhanced pattern recognition that seeks to understand systemic causes rather than assign blame to external factors.

Future Orientation: Rather than ruminating on past mistakes, resilient learners quickly shift attention to future applications of insights gained from the failure experience.

The Experiment vs. Verdict Mindset

Perhaps the most important distinction for developing marketing resilience is learning to frame failures as experiments rather than verdicts. This isn't just a semantic difference—it represents a fundamental shift in how the brain processes and responds to unexpected results.

Verdict Mindset Characteristics

- Treats campaign results as judgments about personal competence or professional worth
- Experiences failure as evidence of inadequate skill, flawed judgment, or strategic incompetence
- Focuses on avoiding future failures rather than maximizing learning opportunities
- Creates internal pressure for perfect performance that paradoxically increases failure probability
- Leads to increasingly conservative approaches that limit growth and innovation potential

Experiment Mindset Characteristics

- Treats campaign results as information about market dynamics, audience psychology, or execution variables
- Experiences failure as data that improves understanding of what works when and why
- Focuses on optimizing learning velocity rather than minimizing failure frequency
- Creates internal permission for intelligent risk-taking that enables breakthrough discoveries
- Leads to increasingly sophisticated approaches that improve both learning and performance

The shift from verdict to experiment mindset doesn't happen through willpower alone—it requires systematic development of what psychologists call "cognitive flexibility" and what we might term "experimental consciousness."

Netflix's Adaptive Intelligence

Netflix's evolution from a DVD rental service to a streaming platform to a content producer provides an extended case study in how an experimental mindset enables adaptation through multiple industry disruptions. Their success hasn't come from avoiding failures but from developing superior capabilities for learning from them.

Key Adaptation Principles

Hypothesis-Driven Strategy: Netflix consistently treats strategic decisions as testable hypotheses rather than permanent commitments. When the Qwikster experiment failed, they didn't defend the strategy; instead, they gathered data about why it failed and adjusted accordingly.

Customer Psychology Integration: Rather than just tracking customer behavior, Netflix invests heavily in understanding the psychological and emotional factors that drive entertainment choices. This deeper understanding enables adaptation to changes in customer needs rather than just customer demographics.

Technology-Culture Synthesis: Netflix recognizes that successful streaming requires both technological infrastructure and cultural content creation. Their adaptation strategy addresses both technical capabilities and creative storytelling rather than viewing them as separate challenges.

Long-term Vision with Short-term Flexibility: Netflix maintains a consistent long-term direction (becoming the premier global entertainment platform) while remaining extremely flexible about tactical approaches, business models, and strategic partnerships.

Data-Intuition Integration: Netflix combines sophisticated data analytics with creative intuition about content and customer experience. Their adaptation decisions emerge from both quantitative analysis and qualitative cultural understanding.

Failure Celebration Culture: Netflix has institutionalized the treatment of intelligent failures as valuable learning experiences rather than career-limiting mistakes. This cultural norm enables faster adaptation because people share insights from failures rather than hiding them.

The Components of Marketing Resilience

Developing the kind of resilience that enables sustained excellence through inevitable challenges requires building several interconnected capabilities that support both learning and performance under pressure.

Emotional Regulation: The ability to maintain emotional equilibrium during failure experiences, preventing amygdala hijack while remaining emotionally engaged with the learning opportunity. This isn't about suppressing emotions but about experiencing them without being overwhelmed.

Cognitive Flexibility: The mental agility to consider multiple explanations for unexpected results, shift perspectives when new information emerges, and adapt frameworks when existing approaches prove inadequate. This includes comfort with ambiguity and uncertainty.

Identity Diversification: Maintaining a sense of professional worth that's not entirely dependent on marketing performance. Resilient marketers typically have multiple sources of identity and competence that provide stability when any single area faces challenges.

Learning Orientation: Genuine curiosity about improvement that's stronger than ego protection needs. This includes actively seeking disconfirming evidence, welcoming challenging feedback, and treating expertise as something to be developed rather than defended.

Systemic Thinking: The ability to see failures within broader contexts rather than as isolated incidents. This includes understanding market dynamics, competitive pressures, and cultural shifts that influence campaign performance beyond individual competence.

Future Focus: The capacity to quickly shift attention from failure analysis to future application, spending just enough time understanding what happened to inform better decisions without getting trapped in rumination or regret.

Practical Resilience Development

Building marketing resilience requires specific practices that strengthen your capacity to learn from difficulties while maintaining both effectiveness and authenticity under pressure.

The Post-Campaign Learning Protocol

Immediately after any significant campaign concludes—whether successful or not—conduct a structured learning review that captures insights while they're still fresh:

- **What worked exactly as expected?** (Confirms existing understanding)
- **What worked better than expected?** (Reveals hidden strengths or market opportunities)
- **What worked worse than expected?** (Identifies areas for improvement or market misunderstandings)
- **What didn't work at all?** (Provides clear feedback about ineffective approaches)
- **What would we do differently?** (Translates insights into actionable future improvements)
- **What questions does this experience raise?** (Identifies areas for deeper investigation)

The Failure Resume Technique

Maintain a documented record of professional failures and the specific insights gained from each. This practice serves multiple functions: it normalizes failure as part of professional development, it creates a reference library of learning experiences, and it demonstrates to yourself that failures consistently contribute to improved performance over time.

The Experimental Planning Method

Before launching campaigns, explicitly identify the hypotheses being tested, the metrics that will provide learning regardless of commercial outcome, and the decision criteria for continuing, modifying, or abandoning approaches based on results. This pre-commitment to experimental thinking makes it easier to maintain a learning orientation when results are disappointing.

The Perspective Diversification Practice

Regularly seek input from people with different professional backgrounds, industry experience, and cultural perspectives when analyzing campaign results. External viewpoints often reveal insights that are invisible from within your own professional context and cognitive frameworks.

The Rapid Recovery Routine

Develop a systematic process for quickly regaining equilibrium after failures: engage in physical activities to discharge stress, practice reflection to restore perspective, and plan activities to redirect attention toward future opportunities rather than past disappointments.

Adaptability in Changing Markets

While resilience helps you recover from individual failures, adaptability enables you to thrive through systematic market changes that require fundamental shifts in approach rather than just tactical adjustments. The marketing landscape has experienced unprecedented change over the past decade, and the pace of disruption continues accelerating.

Characteristics of Highly Adaptable Marketers

Trend Integration Capability: The ability to distinguish between temporary fads and lasting shifts, integrating new platforms, technologies, and cultural changes without abandoning proven principles of human psychology and authentic communication.

Core-Peripheral Flexibility: Maintaining stable core values and fundamental approaches while remaining extremely flexible about peripheral tactics, channels, and execution strategies.

Learning Velocity: Developing new competencies quickly enough to stay relevant in changing markets without sacrificing depth of expertise in areas that remain important.

Comfortable Incompetence: Accepting that rapid market changes will regularly place you in situations where you're temporarily incompetent, viewing this as normal rather than threatening.

Collaborative Adaptation: Building networks and partnerships that provide access to emerging capabilities rather than trying to develop every new competency internally.

The Innovation-Adaptation Balance

One of the most challenging aspects of marketing adaptability is balancing innovation leadership with responsive adaptation. Leading markets requires anticipating changes before they become obvious, while adapting to markets requires responding effectively to changes that have already occurred.

Innovation Leadership Approach

- Invests in understanding emerging technologies, cultural shifts, and demographic changes before they affect mainstream markets
- Experiments with new approaches when the potential upside is significant, even if the probability of success is uncertain
- Accepts higher failure rates in exchange for occasional breakthrough innovations that create competitive advantage
- Focuses on creating new market categories rather than just improving performance in existing categories

Responsive Adaptation Approach

- Monitors market leaders and early adopters to identify successful innovations worth adopting
- Implements proven approaches with superior execution rather than pioneering untested methods
- Minimizes failure rates by learning from others' mistakes and building on others' successes
- Focuses on optimizing performance in existing market categories rather than creating new ones

The most successful marketers develop capabilities for both approaches, knowing when to lead and when to follow based on their specific market position, resource constraints, and strategic objectives.

Building Organizational Adaptability

While individual resilience and adaptability are important, achieving a sustainable competitive advantage requires building these capabilities organizationally, rather than relying on individual traits that might not transfer or scale.

Organizational Resilience Infrastructure

Psychological Safety Culture: Creating environments where people can report failures, share mistakes, and propose controversial ideas without fear of punishment or marginalization.

Experimental Budgeting: Allocating specific resources for testing new approaches with explicit expectation that many experiments will fail while contributing to organizational learning.

Cross-Functional Learning: Ensuring that insights from failures and successes in one area of the organization quickly transfer to other relevant areas rather than remaining in departmental silos.

Leadership Modeling: Having organizational leaders demonstrate experimental thinking, acknowledge their own failures publicly, and celebrate intelligent risk-taking even when it doesn't produce immediate success.

Long-term Patience: Maintaining commitment to adaptation and learning even when short-term performance suffers, recognizing that building adaptive capability requires investment that may not pay off immediately.

The Future of Marketing Adaptability

As artificial intelligence, social media algorithms, consumer behavior, and competitive landscapes continue evolving at an accelerating pace, the ability to adapt quickly while maintaining authentic value creation becomes increasingly crucial for marketing success.

The marketers who will thrive in this environment are those who develop what we might call "conscious adaptability"—the ability to change approaches rapidly without losing sight of fundamental principles, to experiment continuously without sacrificing authentic voice, and to learn from failures without losing confidence in their core competencies.

This requires moving beyond viewing adaptability as merely tactical flexibility to seeing it as strategic consciousness—the ability to maintain both responsiveness and integrity while navigating unprecedented levels of market complexity and change.

The Integration of Resilience and Service

At the highest level, marketing resilience becomes inseparable from commitment to authentic service. When your primary orientation is creating genuine value for your audience, failures become information about how to serve more effectively rather than threats to professional identity. When adaptability is motivated by a deeper understanding of customer needs rather than just competitive positioning, changes feel like evolution rather than abandonment of core principles.

This service orientation doesn't diminish professional ambition—it provides a stable foundation that enables greater risk-taking, more authentic innovation, and more rapid learning because the fundamental purpose remains constant even as methods evolve.

When resilience and adaptability are grounded in authentic service, they become sustainable competitive advantages that compound over time rather than reactive capabilities that create stress and uncertainty. The goal is not just to survive market changes but to thrive through them by consistently finding new ways to serve genuine human needs more effectively.

This integration of resilience, adaptability, and service forms the foundation for marketing mastery that sustains both commercial success and personal fulfillment through the inevitable challenges and changes of professional development. In our final section, we'll explore how these capabilities combine to create the winning mindset that transforms marketing from technique into art, from work into calling.

PART V: THE WINNING MINDSET

Part V

The Winning Mindset

Throughout this journey, we've explored the psychology of marketing consciousness from multiple perspectives—the internal dynamics that govern creative and strategic thinking, the neurological realities that shape how audiences receive and respond to marketing messages, the psychological principles underlying campaigns that capture attention and create lasting influence, and the practical capabilities required to translate understanding into consistent mastery.

Now we arrive at the synthesis: How do all these insights integrate into what we might call the "winning mindset"—a way of being and working that transcends technique to become art, that serves both commercial objectives and authentic human needs so effectively that success feels inevitable rather than effortful?

This winning mindset isn't about adopting new strategies or learning additional techniques. It's about achieving a fundamental transformation in how you relate to marketing work itself—moving from seeing marketing as something you do to experiencing it as something you are, from viewing campaigns as external challenges to be conquered to understanding them as natural expressions of your deepest professional capabilities.

Part V explores this transformation through three essential dimensions: the development of flow states and presence that enable peak performance, the transcendence of traditional competitive thinking toward collaborative value creation, and the integration of marketing practice with lifelong learning and authentic self-expression.

Beyond Technique: The Territory of Mastery

In every complex skill domain—from athletics to music to surgical practice—there comes a point where accumulated technique must transform into something more integrated and intuitive. Musicians stop thinking about individual notes and begin expressing pure musicality. Athletes stop analyzing movement mechanics and begin flowing with natural body intelligence. Surgeons stop following procedural checklists and begin responding intuitively to the unique requirements of each operation.

Marketing mastery involves a similar transformation. After developing competence in psychological principles, strategic frameworks, creative processes, and adaptive learning, there comes a point where these capabilities must integrate into unconscious competence—what we might call "marketing consciousness" that operates through sophisticated understanding without being constrained by it.

Characteristics of Integrated Marketing Consciousness

- Strategic thinking enhances rather than competes with creative intuition
- Psychological understanding informs communication without making it feel calculated
- Business objectives align naturally with authentic value creation rather than conflicting with it
- Campaign development feels both effortless and sophisticated, flowing from a genuine understanding rather than forced effort.
- Success emerges from serving audience needs so effectively that commercial results become inevitable byproducts.

This transformation cannot be achieved through additional study or practice alone—it requires what we might call "consciousness development" that goes beyond skill accumulation to encompass fundamental shifts in identity, purpose, and relationship to work itself.

The Flow State Revolution in Marketing

Psychologist Mihaly Csikszentmihalyi's research on flow states—periods of optimal experience characterized by complete absorption, effortless concentration, and intrinsic motivation—has profound implications for marketing practice that extend far beyond individual performance enhancement.

When marketers achieve flow states consistently, several remarkable phenomena occur:

Creative-Analytical Integration: The traditional tension between analytical rigor and creative freedom disappears. Strategic thinking becomes a natural support system for authentic expression rather than a constraint on it.

Audience Connection Amplification: Flow states enhance empathy and social intelligence, enabling deeper understanding of audience psychology and more authentic communication that feels genuinely helpful rather than manipulative.

Confidence Transmission: The neurological state of flow naturally transmits confidence and authenticity to audiences through subtle cues that operate below conscious awareness but above the level of technique.

Effortless Optimization: Instead of forcing optimization through conscious control, marketing elements naturally align for maximum effectiveness because they emerge from integrated understanding rather than fragmented analysis.

Sustainable Performance: Flow-based marketing creates energy rather than depleting it, enabling sustained high performance without the burnout that often accompanies effortful approaches.

But perhaps most importantly, marketing flow states create what can only be described as "collaborative consciousness"—a state where serving audience needs and achieving business objectives become indistinguishable because both emerge from the same authentic understanding of human value creation.

Beyond Competition: The Collaborative Paradigm

Traditional marketing thinking operates within a competitive paradigm—win-lose dynamics where your success requires your competitors' failure, where customer attention is a scarce resource to be captured, where market share represents territory to be conquered through superior force or strategy.

The winning mindset represents a fundamental shift toward what we might call the "collaborative paradigm"—win-win dynamics where your success enhances rather than diminishes others' opportunities, where customer attention is earned through authentic value creation, and where market leadership emerges from expanding possibilities rather than controlling existing ones.

Competitive Paradigm Characteristics

- Views marketing as warfare where competitors are enemies to be defeated
- Focuses on capturing market share from existing competitors
- Creates value by convincing customers to choose your offering instead of alternatives
- Measures success primarily through relative positioning against other brands
- Generates stress and anxiety because success depends partly on factors outside your control

Collaborative Paradigm Characteristics

- Views marketing as a service where competitors are fellow value creators addressing similar human needs
- Focuses on expanding market categories by serving previously unmet needs
- Creates value by helping customers achieve goals they might not have thought possible
- Measures success primarily through absolute value creation for all stakeholders
- Generates energy and fulfillment because success depends primarily on factors within your control

This shift doesn't mean becoming less competitive in terms of performance standards; rather, it means becoming more collaborative in our fundamental orientation toward market dynamics and human relationships.

The Identity Evolution: From Marketer to Artist

Perhaps the most profound aspect of developing a winning mindset is the gradual shift from viewing yourself as a marketer to seeing your authentic self-expression as naturally taking the form of marketing excellence.

This identity shift transforms everything about how marketing works and feels:

From External Validation to Internal Standards: Instead of measuring success primarily through external approval, recognition, or competitive positioning, you develop internal standards based on authentic value creation and genuine service to audience needs.

From Technique Application to Natural Expression: Instead of applying learned techniques to marketing challenges, you begin expressing natural capabilities that happen to manifest through marketing practice.

From Work-Life Separation to Integrated Living: Instead of viewing marketing as separate from your personal development and authentic interests, you recognize marketing mastery as one expression of your overall growth as a conscious human being.

From Problem-Solving to Opportunity Creation: Instead of seeing marketing primarily as solving business problems or overcoming market challenges, you begin recognizing marketing as creating possibilities that didn't exist before your involvement.

This evolution doesn't happen through deciding to think differently—it emerges naturally from sustained practice of the principles we've explored throughout this book, particularly when that practice is motivated by genuine service rather than just professional advancement.

The Integration of Commercial and Spiritual Success

One of the most important but rarely discussed aspects of marketing mastery is the integration of commercial effectiveness with what we might call "spiritual satisfaction"—the deep fulfillment that comes from work that serves something larger than immediate self-interest.

Traditional business education often treats these as competing values: commercial success requires focusing on profit maximization while spiritual satisfaction requires prioritizing meaning over money. The winning mindset transcends this false choice by recognizing that the most sustainable commercial success emerges from work that genuinely serves human needs and contributes to positive cultural evolution.

Characteristics of Integrated Success

- Commercial results improve as work becomes more aligned with authentic values
- Professional recognition flows naturally from genuine contribution rather than self-promotion
- Financial rewards increase as value creation becomes more authentic and effective
- Personal fulfillment deepens as work becomes more clearly connected to meaningful service
- Long-term sustainability improves as success becomes less dependent on external validation

This integration doesn't require changing your business objectives or compromising professional ambitions; instead, it involves aligning those objectives with deeper purposes that provide intrinsic motivation regardless of external circumstances.

The Ripple Effect: Marketing as Cultural Contribution

When marketing is practiced from the winning mindset, it transcends purely commercial objectives to become a form of cultural contribution. Instead of just selling products or services, marketing becomes a way of enhancing the cultural environment, elevating public discourse, and contributing to the development of collective consciousness.

Cultural Contribution Characteristics

- Creates marketing that people actively seek out rather than passively tolerate
- Generates brand relationships that customers feel grateful to have discovered
- Produces communication that enhances rather than pollutes the information environment
- Builds community around shared values rather than just shared consumption
- Influences industry standards toward more authentic and service-oriented practices

This cultural dimension of marketing mastery creates what economists call "positive externalities"—benefits that extend beyond the immediate commercial transaction to serve broader social good. When marketing operates at this level, it becomes a force for cultural evolution rather than just commercial persuasion.

The Practice Integration: Marketing as Spiritual Path

At the highest level, marketing practice becomes indistinguishable from spiritual practice—not in any religious sense, but in the sense of work that consistently develops consciousness, serves authentic human needs, and contributes to the greater good while also achieving practical objectives.

Marketing as Spiritual Practice Characteristics

- Every campaign becomes an opportunity for learning and growth rather than just a business objective
- Professional challenges become occasions for developing patience, creativity, and resilience rather than just obstacles to overcome
- Success and failure both contribute equally to the development of consciousness rather than being purely positive or negative experiences.
- Work relationships become opportunities for authentic connection and mutual service rather than just professional networking.
- Long-term career development focuses on contribution and consciousness rather than just advancement and accumulation.

This perspective doesn't require abandoning professional ambition or commercial objectives—it provides a framework that supports both worldly success and personal development through the same activities.

The Invitation to Transformation

Part V explores how to cultivate this winning mindset through three essential practices: developing the presence and flow states that enable peak performance, transcending competitive thinking toward collaborative value creation, and integrating marketing practice with lifelong learning and authentic self-expression.

This isn't about becoming a different kind of marketer—it's about becoming more fully yourself while expressing that authenticity through marketing excellence. The winning mindset emerges not from adopting new beliefs or techniques but from removing the internal obstacles and external pressures that prevent your natural marketing intelligence from expressing itself most effectively.

The transformation we're exploring represents the fruition of everything we've discovered throughout this journey: when psychological understanding integrates with authentic value creation, when strategic thinking serves rather than competes with creative intelligence, when commercial objectives align with genuine human service, something remarkable emerges—marketing that wins not just customers and revenue but hearts and minds, marketing that succeeds not just in immediate objectives but in long-term cultural contribution.

Welcome to the territory of the winning mindset, where marketing excellence becomes a natural expression of consciousness development, where commercial success serves spiritual growth, and where professional mastery contributes to both personal fulfillment and collective flourishing.

The goal isn't just to become better at marketing—it's to become the kind of person whose authentic self-expression naturally takes the form of marketing that serves, inspires, and elevates everyone it touches.

Chapter 13

Presence, Flow, and Marketing Greatness

Neuroscience of flow applied to campaign design—examples: musicians, athletes, and viral brands

On January 28, 1986, millions of Americans watched in horror as the Space Shuttle Challenger exploded 73 seconds after launch, killing all seven crew members aboard. In the immediate aftermath, as the nation struggled to process the tragedy, President Ronald Reagan was scheduled to deliver the State of the Union address that evening. Instead, he made a decision that would create one of the most memorable and healing moments in American political communication.

Speaking directly to the camera from the Oval Office, Reagan abandoned his prepared remarks and delivered what became known as the Challenger Address. In just over four minutes, he managed to acknowledge the nation's grief, honor the fallen astronauts, provide comfort to families and children watching, and reaffirm America's commitment to space exploration. The speech felt completely natural and unrehearsed, yet every word, pause, and inflection seemed perfectly calibrated to serve the moment's emotional needs.

What made this communication so powerful wasn't just Reagan's skill as a communicator—it was his ability to be completely present to the moment, fully absorbing the nation's emotional state and responding from a place of genuine understanding rather than political calculation. He achieved what psychologists call a "flow state"—complete absorption in the task at hand, where self-consciousness disappears and performance becomes effortless, intuitive, and seemingly perfect.

This represents marketing and communication at its highest level: presence so complete that authentic understanding naturally transforms into effortless effectiveness, where serving the audience's genuine needs becomes indistinguishable from achieving your own objectives.

The Neuroscience of Marketing Flow States

Flow states in marketing creation and execution involve specific neurological patterns that differ dramatically from the brain activity associated with effortful, anxious, or self-conscious performance. Understanding these patterns provides insight into how to access and sustain the mental states that produce marketing greatness.

Neurological Characteristics of Marketing Flow

Transient Hypofrontality: The brain's prefrontal cortex—responsible for self-criticism, social anxiety, and analytical overthinking—downregulates during flow states. This creates temporary freedom from the internal critic that often interferes with authentic creative expression.

Enhanced Default Mode Network Activity: The brain regions associated with insight, creativity, and unconscious processing become more active and integrated, enabling the kind of breakthrough thinking that produces original approaches to familiar challenges.

Increased Alpha Wave Production: The brain generates more alpha waves, associated with relaxed awareness and creative thinking, while maintaining enough beta wave activity to enable focused execution.

Heightened Dopamine and Norepinephrine: These neurochemicals enhance focus, pattern recognition, and motivation while reducing the sense of effort required to maintain attention and execute complex tasks.

Reduced Amygdala Activity: The brain's alarm system becomes less active, reducing anxiety and defensive responses that can interfere with authentic communication and creative risk-taking.

Enhanced Neural Connectivity: Different brain regions communicate more effectively with each other, enabling the integration of analytical thinking, creative insight, emotional intelligence, and social awareness that characterizes great marketing.

These neurological patterns explain why marketing created in flow states feels both effortless to create and natural to experience—the brain is operating in its optimal state for complex, creative, socially-aware performance.

The Conditions for Marketing Flow

Flow states cannot be forced, but they can be cultivated by creating conditions that support the neurological patterns associated with optimal performance. For marketers, this requires understanding both internal psychological conditions and external environmental factors that either support or interfere with flow state access.

Internal Flow Conditions

Clear Intent Without Attachment: Having definite objectives for your marketing while remaining unattached to specific outcomes. This paradoxical state enables focused effort without the anxiety that comes from trying to control results.

Challenge-Skill Balance: Working on projects that stretch your capabilities without overwhelming them. Flow occurs at the intersection of meaningful challenge and genuine competence.

Present-Moment Awareness: Focus entirely on current creative and strategic tasks rather than ruminating about past campaigns or worrying about future performance.

Intrinsic Motivation: Engaging with marketing challenges because they're inherently interesting and valuable rather than just pursuing external rewards or avoiding negative consequences.

Authentic Expression: Creating marketing that emerges from genuine understanding and sincere desire to serve rather than performing roles or adopting voices that feel foreign to your natural communication style.

External Flow Conditions

Minimal Distractions: Physical and digital environments that support sustained attention rather than fragmenting it across multiple inputs.

Psychological Safety: Organizational cultures that support creative risk-taking without fear of punishment for intelligent failures or unconventional approaches.

Sufficient Resources: Access to the tools, information, and support needed to execute your creative vision without unnecessary friction or limitation.

Collaborative Energy: Working relationships that enhance rather than drain creative energy, with colleagues who contribute to rather than detract from optimal performance states.

Time Protection: Sufficient uninterrupted time to develop ideas fully, rather than constantly starting and stopping creative processes due to meeting schedules or urgent requests.

Case Study: Musicians and the Flow of Authentic Performance

The music industry provides the clearest examples of how flow states translate into cultural impact and commercial success. Musicians who achieve lasting influence typically demonstrate the ability to access flow states consistently, creating performances that feel both technically excellent and emotionally authentic.

John Coltrane's "A Love Supreme": Recorded in a single session in December 1964, this album emerged from what Coltrane described as a spiritual flow state where musical expression became indistinguishable from religious devotion. The resulting work influenced generations of musicians and continues selling decades after its creation because it captured and transmitted an authentic, transcendent experience.

Aretha Franklin's "Respect": Franklin's 1967 version of Otis Redding's song transformed it from a straightforward plea into a civil rights anthem by channeling her personal experience of dignity and empowerment into musical expression. The performance emerged from complete presence to both the musical material and its cultural moment.

Johnny Cash's "Hurt": Cash's 2002 cover of Nine Inch Nails' song created one of the most powerful musical performances in popular culture by deeply connecting with his own mortality and life experience. The performance succeeded because it emerged from authentic engagement with the material rather than technical reproduction.

Common Flow Characteristics in Musical Greatness

- Complete absorption in the musical material without self-consciousness about performance
- Authentic emotional engagement that transmits to listeners through neurological mirroring
- Technical competence that serves emotional expression rather than competing with it
- Cultural relevance that emerges from genuine personal experience rather than calculated positioning

- Spontaneous elements that couldn't be replicated exactly, even by the same performer

These characteristics translate directly to marketing excellence when campaigns emerge from similar flow states.

Athletic Flow and Marketing Performance

Professional athletes provide another instructive model for how flow states enable peak performance under pressure. The mental states that enable athletic excellence—complete presence, effortless execution, and integrated consciousness—apply directly to marketing challenges that require both strategic thinking and authentic communication.

Michael Jordan's "Flow Zone": Jordan frequently described entering mental states during crucial games where time seemed to slow down, opponents' movements became predictable, and optimal decisions emerged naturally without conscious analysis. This same state enables marketers to access an intuitive understanding of audience psychology and market dynamics that conscious analysis alone cannot provide.

Serena Williams' "Competitive Meditation": Williams developed the ability to maintain meditative awareness during high-pressure matches, enabling her to respond to each point with complete presence rather than being distracted by past mistakes or future consequences. Marketers can develop a similar capacity to remain present to current campaign requirements rather than being overwhelmed by performance anxiety or outcome attachment.

Tom Brady's "Pocket Presence": Brady's ability to remain calm and aware under intense pressure from defensive rushers mirrors the marketing challenge of maintaining authentic communication amid competitive pressures, tight deadlines, and performance expectations.

Athletic Flow Principles for Marketing

- Training and preparation create the competence foundation that enables flow during performance
- Being present-moment aware during execution prevents past failures or future concerns from interfering with current performance.
- Trust in unconscious competence allows natural abilities to operate without conscious interference.
- Focus on process rather than outcomes reduces anxiety while paradoxically improving results.

- Integration of technical skill with authentic expression creates performance that transcends pure competence.

Viral Brands and the Flow of Cultural Resonance

Some brands achieve what can only be described as "cultural flow states"—periods where their communication becomes so aligned with collective cultural needs and consciousness that viral adoption feels inevitable rather than manufactured.

Old Spice's "The Man Your Man Could Smell Like" Campaign (2010): This campaign achieved viral success by accessing perfect cultural timing—simultaneously parodying and celebrating masculine stereotypes in ways that felt both humorous and affirming. The creators appeared to be in a flow state with cultural consciousness, creating content that felt both spontaneous and sophisticated.

Dove's "Real Beauty" Campaign (2004-present): Dove's long-running campaign tapped into cultural flow around changing beauty standards and female empowerment. Rather than creating artificial movements, they amplified conversations that were already emerging in collective consciousness, making their brand a natural part of cultural evolution.

Nike's "Just Do It" Philosophy (1988-present): Nike achieved cultural flow by aligning their brand with universal human psychology around motivation and self-overcoming. The campaign works across cultures and generations because it connects with fundamental aspects of human aspiration rather than temporary cultural trends.

Airbnb's "Belong Anywhere" Vision (2008-present): Airbnb's brand emergence coincided with cultural shifts toward authentic travel experiences and sharing economy values. Their success emerged from recognizing and serving cultural needs that were already emerging rather than trying to create artificial demand.

Characteristics of Cultural Flow States

- Brand messaging aligns with existing but unexpressed cultural needs
- Communication feels like a natural expression of collective consciousness rather than external persuasion
- Viral adoption occurs through genuine enthusiasm rather than incentivized sharing

- Cultural impact extends beyond immediate commercial objectives to influence broader conversations
- Long-term brand strength emerges from authentic cultural contribution rather than just marketing effectiveness

Practical Flow State Development for Marketers

Developing consistent access to flow states requires systematic practice that addresses both internal psychological development and external environmental design. This isn't about occasional peak experiences but about building capacity for sustained optimal performance.

Daily Flow Practices

Morning Centering Ritual: Begin each day with practices that establish present-moment awareness and clear intention—meditation, journaling, physical exercise, or other activities that create mental clarity and emotional equilibrium.

Single-Task Focus Sessions: Regularly practice sustained attention to individual marketing tasks without multitasking or digital distraction. Start with 25-30 minute sessions and gradually extend to longer periods.

Creative Flow Blocks: Schedule specific times for creative work when you're least likely to be interrupted, typically matching your natural energy rhythms rather than forcing creativity during low-energy periods.

Preparation-Execution Separation: Thoroughly prepare for marketing projects during designated planning times, then execute during separate sessions where you trust your preparation and focus entirely on present-moment performance.

Regular Skill Development: Continuously build marketing competencies through study, practice, and experimentation so that technical capabilities support rather than limit flow state access.

Reflection and Integration: Conclude work sessions with a brief reflection on what enabled or hindered flow states, fostering self-awareness to enhance future flow access.

Environmental Flow Design

Physical Space Optimization: Create work environments that support sustained attention and creative thinking—appropriate lighting, comfortable furniture, minimal visual clutter, and easy access to necessary tools.

Digital Environment Curation: Design digital workspaces that eliminate unnecessary notifications, distractions, and cognitive overhead that fragment attention during creative work.

Boundary Protection: Establish clear boundaries around flow time that protect sustained attention from interruptions, urgent requests, and non-essential communications.

Collaborative Flow Conditions: When working with teams, establish group norms that support collective flow states—clear objectives, defined roles, efficient decision-making processes, and shared commitment to excellence.

The Integration of Flow and Strategy

One of the most important distinctions for marketing professionals is learning to integrate flow states with strategic rigor rather than viewing them as competing approaches. The highest level of marketing performance emerges when analytical thinking and intuitive flow support rather than interfere with each other.

Pre-Flow Strategic Preparation: Use analytical thinking to establish clear campaign objectives, understand audience psychology, research the competitive landscape, and identify key constraints and opportunities before entering creative flow states.

Flow-Based Execution: During creative and strategic development, trust unconscious competence to integrate prepared information into optimal solutions rather than trying to control every element of the creative process consciously.

Post-Flow Analytical Refinement: After initial creative development in flow states, use analytical thinking to refine, test, and optimize approaches while preserving the essential qualities that emerged from flow-based creation.

Iterative Flow-Strategy Cycles: Develop marketing projects through alternating cycles of flow-based creation and analytical refinement rather than trying to maintain either state continuously throughout the entire process.

This integration creates marketing that combines the authenticity and effectiveness of flow states with the strategic sophistication of rigorous analytical thinking.

The Transmission Effect: Flow as Influence

Perhaps the most remarkable aspect of marketing created in flow states is its neurological contagiousness. When marketing emerges from genuine flow consciousness, audiences unconsciously detect and respond to the neurological authenticity, creating influence that feels natural rather than manipulative.

Flow Transmission Mechanisms

Mirror Neuron Activation: Audiences' mirror neurons respond to the neurological authenticity of flow-based communication, creating sympathetic activation of similar brain states in receivers.

Reduced Resistance: Marketing created in flow states triggers fewer defensive responses because it emerges from genuine service intention rather than a manipulative agenda.

Enhanced Believability: The congruence between conscious message and unconscious intention that characterizes flow communication creates immediate credibility that conscious persuasion cannot replicate.

Emotional Resonance: Flow states enable authentic emotional expression that activates corresponding emotions in audiences through neurological mirroring systems.

Cultural Attunement: Marketing created in flow with cultural consciousness feels timely and relevant in ways that researched positioning often cannot achieve.

Beyond Individual Flow: Organizational Flow States

While individual flow states are important, sustainable marketing excellence requires building organizational capabilities for collective flow—team and company-wide states that enable collaborative creation at the highest level.

Organizational Flow Characteristics

- Shared vision that creates unified direction without stifling individual creativity
- Collaborative processes that enhance rather than diminish individual flow access
- Cultural norms that support risk-taking, experimentation, and authentic expression
- Leadership that models flow consciousness and creates conditions for others to access similar states
- Systems and structures that support rather than interfere with optimal performance conditions

When organizations achieve collective flow states, they often produce marketing campaigns that feel culturally inevitable—communication that seems to emerge naturally from cultural needs rather than being imposed through strategic force.

The Future of Flow-Based Marketing

As artificial intelligence handles increasingly sophisticated analytical tasks, the competitive advantage for human marketers will shift toward capabilities that AI cannot replicate: flow consciousness, authentic emotional intelligence, cultural intuition, and the ability to create communication that emerges from genuine human understanding and service intention.

The marketers who will thrive in this environment are those who develop mastery of flow states not as occasional peak experiences but as accessible resources. These resources can be cultivated systematically and applied consistently to create marketing that serves both commercial objectives and authentic human needs.

When marketing consistently emerges from flow consciousness, something remarkable happens: the boundary between marketer and audience, between commercial communication and authentic service, between business success and cultural contribution begins to dissolve. The marketing becomes a natural expression of consciousness development that serves everyone it touches.

This represents marketing at its highest potential—not just effective communication. Still, conscious communication that elevates both creator and receiver serves both immediate objectives and long-term cultural evolution and demonstrates how commercial excellence and spiritual development can become mutually reinforcing rather than competing forces.

In our next chapter, we'll explore how this individual and organizational flow consciousness enables the transcendence of traditional competitive thinking toward collaborative approaches that create value for entire market ecosystems.

Chapter 14

Beyond Competition: Creating Category Kings

The brain's need for newness—case: Tesla redefining electric vehicles

In 2008, when Elon Musk unveiled the Tesla Roadster at a price point of $109,000, every automotive industry expert knew exactly what category it belonged to: electric vehicles. The category had existed for over a century, populated by underpowered golf carts, experimental prototypes, and earnest but uninspiring economy cars that screamed environmental compromise to anyone within a hundred yards.

But something extraordinary happened in the decade that followed. Tesla didn't just succeed in the electric vehicle category—they fundamentally redefined what that category could mean. Instead of competing for market share in the existing "efficient but compromised" electric vehicle space, they created an entirely new mental category: "electric vehicles as the future of automotive excellence."

By 2022, Tesla had achieved something unprecedented in automotive history: it had higher profit margins than luxury traditional automakers. It was selling significantly more vehicles than most established brands, all while transforming the entire automotive industry's vision of its own future. They had become what business strategists call a "category king"—not just the leading player in a category, but the company that defines what the category itself means.

This achievement illustrates perhaps the most important insight about transcending competition: the biggest opportunities don't come from winning existing games but from changing the game itself. When you create new mental categories rather than competing in existing ones, the brain's fundamental need for novelty and progress works for you rather than against you.

The Neuroscience of Category Creation

Understanding how new categories form in consumer consciousness requires examining how the brain processes and organizes information about products, services, and brands. The human mind doesn't experience markets as collections of individual offerings—it experiences them as organized categories that enable rapid decision-making and social communication.

Neurological Category Formation

Pattern Recognition Systems: The brain automatically groups similar products and services into categories to reduce cognitive load. When encountering new offerings, it first attempts to fit them into existing categories before creating new ones.

Novelty Detection Networks: Specialized brain regions constantly scan for information that doesn't fit existing patterns. Truly novel categories activate these networks, creating heightened attention and enhanced memory formation.

Social Categorization Integration: Category formation is heavily influenced by social proof and cultural consensus. Categories become "real" when enough people begin using them in social communication and decision-making.

Future Simulation Activation: New categories that suggest improved future possibilities activate the brain's default mode network, creating positive anticipation and emotional investment in category development.

Identity Integration Systems: Categories that align with personal identity and social positioning receive enhanced processing priority and become more resistant to competitive displacement.

Tesla succeeded because they activated all these systems simultaneously: they created genuine novelty that couldn't be easily categorized, provided social proof through early adopter enthusiasm, suggested a compelling future vision, and aligned with evolving identity aspirations around environmental consciousness and technological sophistication.

Beyond Market Share: The Category Design Paradigm

Traditional competitive strategy focuses on gaining market share within existing categories—becoming the best electric vehicle, the leading social media platform, or the top productivity software. Category design represents a fundamentally different approach: creating new categories where traditional competitive dynamics don't yet exist.

Market Share Competitive Dynamics

- Zero-sum game where your success requires competitors' failure
- Focus on incremental improvements to existing value propositions
- Competition based on features, pricing, and positioning within established frameworks
- Success measured by the percentage of the existing market captured
- Customer acquisition through persuading people to switch from their current solutions

Category Design Dynamics

- Positive-sum game where category growth benefits all early participants
- Focus on fundamental redefinition of what's possible or desirable
- Competition based on vision, cultural leadership, and category evangelism
- Success measured by category growth and definitional authority
- Customer acquisition through expanding market consciousness rather than switching behavior

The shift from market share to category design changes everything about how marketing works. Instead of convincing customers to choose you over alternatives, you help them understand why this new category deserves their attention.

Tesla's Category Redefinition Mastery

Tesla's transformation of the electric vehicle category provides perhaps the most instructive case study in modern category design. Their success came not from building better electric cars within existing category definitions, but from systematically redefining what electric vehicles could represent.

Traditional Electric Vehicle Category (Pre-Tesla)

- **Primary value proposition**: Environmental responsibility through reduced emissions
- **Target audience**: Environmentally conscious consumers willing to accept performance compromises
- **Key messaging**: Efficient, responsible, practical transportation
- **Competitive positioning**: Alternative to gas vehicles for specific use cases
- **Cultural meaning**: Sacrifice performance for environmental benefit

Tesla's Redefined Category

- **Primary value proposition**: Technological superiority and automotive excellence that happens to be electric
- **Target audience**: Performance and technology enthusiasts who also care about environmental impact
- **Key messaging**: The future of automotive technology, available today
- **Competitive positioning**: Superior to all vehicles regardless of power source
- **Cultural meaning**: Progressive leadership and technological sophistication

Strategic Category Redefinition Elements

Performance Redefinition: Instead of positioning electric as efficient but slower, Tesla demonstrated electric as faster than traditional performance cars. The Roadster's 0-60 mph time of 3.7 seconds shattered assumptions about electric vehicle capabilities.

Luxury Repositioning: Rather than targeting economy or mid-market segments, Tesla entered at the luxury level, making electric vehicles aspirational rather than compromised.

Technology Integration: Tesla positioned their vehicles as computers with wheels rather than cars that happen to be electric, emphasizing software capabilities, autonomous features, and continuous updates.

Infrastructure Creation: Instead of accepting existing charging limitations, Tesla built a proprietary charging network that made electric ownership more convenient than traditional vehicle ownership for many use cases.

Cultural Leadership: Tesla became advocates for sustainable technology broadly rather than just electric vehicles specifically, positioning themselves as leaders in civilizational progress rather than just automotive innovation.

Ecosystem Expansion: Tesla expanded beyond vehicles into energy storage, solar panels, and autonomous driving, reinforcing their position as comprehensive sustainable technology leaders rather than just car manufacturers.

The Brain's Need for Newness and Progress

Human beings possess what neuroscientists call "neophilia"—a fundamental attraction to novelty that served evolutionary survival but now drives consumer behavior in complex ways. Understanding this psychological reality is crucial for category design because new categories must satisfy both rational utility and emotional novelty needs.

Neurological Novelty Processing

Dopamine Activation: Genuinely new categories trigger dopamine release associated with anticipation and reward prediction, creating positive emotional associations before conscious evaluation occurs.

Curiosity Drive: Novel categories activate information-seeking behaviors as the brain attempts to understand and categorize new possibilities, generating engagement that existing categories cannot match.

Status Signaling Opportunity: Early adoption of new categories provides social differentiation opportunities that established categories cannot offer, creating additional motivation for engagement.

Future Orientation: New categories enable people to imagine improved future versions of themselves and their lives, activating aspirational psychology that drives premium pricing acceptance.

Learning Pleasure: Mastering new categories provides intrinsic satisfaction from developing competence, which incremental improvements within existing categories rarely generate.

Tesla succeeded because it satisfied all these novelty needs while delivering genuine utility improvements, creating category adoption that felt both rationally justified and emotionally rewarding.

Case Study: Other Category Kings

Tesla's category redefinition success isn't unique—other companies have achieved similar transformations by transcending traditional competitive dynamics to create new mental categories.

Netflix: From DVD Rental to Entertainment Platform

- **Traditional category**: Video rental competing with Blockbuster on convenience and pricing
- **Redefined category:** Personalized entertainment platform that learns and recommends
- **Key insight**: People don't want to rent movies; they want effortless access to entertainment that matches their preferences
- **Neurological appeal**: Reduced decision fatigue plus personalized discovery, plus binge-watching enablement

Uber: From Taxi Alternative to Transportation Platform

- **Traditional category**: Alternative taxi service competing on price and availability
- **Redefined category**: On-demand transportation platform enabling new urban mobility
- **Key insight**: People don't want to hail taxis; they want transportation that feels as convenient as their personal vehicle
- **Neurological appeal**: Reduced uncertainty plus status signaling plus technology empowerment

Airbnb: From Budget Accommodation to Authentic Travel

- **Traditional category**: Budget alternative to hotels competing on price
- **Redefined category**: Authentic local experiences enabling "belonging anywhere"
- **Key insight**: People don't just want places to sleep; they want to experience destinations like locals

- **Neurological appeal**: Novelty seeking plus community connection plus identity expression

Peloton: From Exercise Equipment to Fitness Community

- **Traditional category**: Home exercise equipment competing on features and price
- **Redefined category**: Connected fitness community enabling home workout experiences that rival premium gyms
- **Key insight**: People don't want exercise equipment; they want motivating fitness experiences
- **Neurological appeal**: Social connection plus gamification plus convenience optimization

Common Category King Characteristics

- Identify unmet psychological needs that existing categories don't address
- Create new value propositions that make traditional comparisons irrelevant
- Build ecosystems that reinforce category definition rather than just offering products
- Establish cultural leadership that influences industry evolution
- Generate network effects that strengthen category position over time

The Psychology of Category Evangelism

Creating new categories requires more than product innovation—it requires what we might call "category evangelism," the ability to help potential customers understand and adopt new mental frameworks for thinking about their needs and possible solutions.

Effective Category Evangelism Elements

Problem Redefinition: Instead of solving existing problems better, help people recognize problems they didn't know they had or couldn't articulate clearly.

Future Vision Creation: Paint compelling pictures of how life or work could be different when this new category becomes widely adopted.

Social Proof Acceleration: Create early adopter communities that provide social validation for category adoption rather than just product purchase.

Educational Content Leadership: Become the primary source of information about this new category rather than just promoting your specific offering within it.

Cultural Trend Alignment: Position category adoption as alignment with broader cultural shifts rather than just individual consumer choice.

Identity Integration: Help early adopters understand how participating in a category enhances rather than conflicts with their existing identity and values.

Tesla excelled at category evangelism by consistently communicating that adopting electric vehicles was part of humanity's sustainable energy transition, rather than just an individual transportation choice. This elevated category adoption from consumer decision to cultural contribution.

The Network Effects of Category Creation

Successful category creation generates what economists call "network effects"—phenomena where value increases as more people participate in the category. These effects create sustainable competitive advantages that pure product innovation cannot achieve.

Types of Category Network Effects

Supply-Side Networks: More category participants attract more suppliers, partners, and supporting infrastructure, improving the overall category experience.

Demand-Side Networks: Larger user bases create better experiences for individual users through increased social proof, content generation, and feature development.

Data Network Effects: Increased category usage generates better data, enabling improved product development and customer experience optimization.

Developer/Partner Networks: Successful categories attract third-party innovation that enhances value without requiring direct investment from category creators.

Cultural Network Effects: Widespread category adoption creates social norms and expectations that reinforce continued growth and evolution.

Tesla built all these network effects: their success attracted investment in charging infrastructure, created enthusiast communities, generated driving data that improved autonomous capabilities, encouraged third-party accessories and services, and established electric vehicles as symbols of progressive thinking.

The Collaborative Approach to Competition

Category kings don't eliminate competition—they redefine what competition means. Instead of zero-sum battles for market share, they create positive-sum environments where category growth benefits all participants while establishing themselves as definitional leaders.

Traditional Competitive Dynamics

- Focus on defending the market position against direct competitors
- View competitor success as a threat to your success
- Compete primarily on features, pricing, and marketing execution
- Measure success through relative market share performance
- Create adversarial relationships with industry peers

Category King Competitive Dynamics

- Focus on expanding category awareness and adoption
- View early competitor success as validation of category potential
- Compete primarily on vision, culture, and category definition
- Measure success through absolute category growth and leadership position
- Create collaborative relationships that advance category development

This collaborative approach enables category kings to benefit from competitor marketing investments that expand category awareness, to establish industry standards that favor their approach, and to build ecosystem partnerships that strengthen their definitional authority.

Practical Category Design Principles

Creating new categories requires the systematic application of specific principles that align with how human brains form new mental categories and adopt new behavioral patterns.

Category Naming and Definition

- Choose names that suggest expanded possibilities rather than just improved versions of existing categories
- Create definitions that highlight psychological benefits rather than just functional features
- Establish category criteria that favor your approach while remaining genuinely valuable
- Develop language and concepts that early adopters can use to explain category value to others

Early Adopter Strategy

- Identify people whose existing pain points make them receptive to category innovation
- Create products and experiences that deliver disproportionate value to these early users
- Build community and communication channels that enable early adopters to influence broader market adoption
- Generate social proof and success stories that demonstrate category value to mainstream audiences

Ecosystem Development

- Build partnerships and infrastructure that support category adoption rather than just product distribution.
- Create educational content and thought leadership that establishes you as a category authority.
- Develop complementary products and services that reinforce category definition.

- Establish industry relationships that accelerate category legitimization and growth.

Cultural Integration

- Align category positioning with broader cultural trends and values rather than just market opportunities.
- Create meaning and purpose that extend beyond immediate customer utility to encompass social contribution.
- Develop a brand narrative that positions category adoption as an expression of identity rather than just a product choice.
- Build communication approaches that feel like cultural contributions rather than just commercial promotions.

The Future of Category Creation

As global markets become more complex and consumer consciousness continues evolving, the ability to create and define new categories becomes increasingly important for sustainable competitive advantage. Traditional product differentiation becomes less sustainable as manufacturing capabilities converge and artificial intelligence automates optimization.

The companies that will dominate the next decade are those that develop capabilities for systematic category innovation—not just better products within existing categories, but fundamentally new ways of thinking about human needs and possible solutions.

Emerging Category Creation Opportunities

- Sustainability-integrated business models that transcend "green" as a separate category
- Human-AI collaboration platforms that redefine productivity and creativity
- Community-commerce integration that transforms retail into a social experience
- Wellbeing-technology synthesis that addresses digital life quality rather than just efficiency
- Localism-globalism balance that enables planetary connection with community rootedness

These opportunities require the kind of consciousness-based marketing we've explored throughout this book: a deep understanding of human psychology, an authentic service orientation, systematic innovation capabilities, and the ability to envision and communicate possibilities that don't yet exist in collective consciousness.

Category Kings as Cultural Leaders

At the highest level, category creation becomes a form of cultural leadership—helping society develop new ways of thinking about persistent challenges and emerging possibilities. Category kings don't just build successful businesses; they contribute to the evolution of collective consciousness in ways that serve both commercial objectives and genuine human development.

This cultural leadership dimension transforms category creation from pure business strategy into what we might call "conscious commerce"—business development that serves both immediate stakeholder needs and long-term cultural evolution.

When category design operates at this level, it transcends traditional marketing to become a form of applied futurism—helping society recognize and adopt possibilities that serve authentic human flourishing rather than just commercial optimization.

In our final chapter, we'll explore how this cultural leadership consciousness integrates with lifelong learning and authentic self-expression to create a marketing practice that sustains both professional excellence and personal fulfillment throughout an entire career.

Chapter 15

The Inner Game as Lifelong Practice

Marketing as both art and self-mastery—final reflections, actionable exercises, and mindset rituals

On his 80th birthday, master potter Kintaro Shimooka was asked by a visitor how it felt to have achieved perfection in his craft. The old artisan smiled gently and gestured toward the simple clay bowl he was forming on his wheel. "Every day," he said, "I am still learning how clay wants to become a bowl. After sixty years, I understand only that I know nothing, and this nothing-knowing is everything."

This response captures something essential about mastery in any complex domain: the moment you believe you have arrived is the moment you begin declining. True expertise isn't a destination but a way of traveling—a commitment to continuous learning, deepening awareness, and authentic engagement with your craft that sustains both excellence and growth throughout an entire career.

Marketing mastery follows the same pattern. The psychological principles we've explored, the neurological insights we've examined, the strategic frameworks we've developed—all of these serve not as final answers but as foundations for lifelong inquiry into how human consciousness works, how authentic communication functions, and how genuine service can be expressed through commercial activity.

The inner game of marketing isn't something you win once and then possess forever. It's a practice you develop, refine, and deepen through every campaign, every challenge, every success, and every failure throughout your professional journey.

The Mastery Paradox: Knowing More, Understanding Less

One of the most profound shifts that occurs as marketing expertise develops is what we might call the "mastery paradox"—the more you learn about how marketing actually works, the more humble you become about how much remains mysterious, unpredictable, and worthy of continued exploration.

Early Career Certainty

- Clear rules and best practices provide a confident framework for decision-making
- Success and failure feel directly related to technique application and the effort level
- Market dynamics seem predictable and responsive to strategic manipulation
- Professional identity builds on accumulated knowledge and proven competencies
- Growth means learning more answers to marketing challenges

Mastery-Level Uncertainty

- Principles guide while acknowledging the complexity that exceeds any framework
- Success and failure reveal themselves as influenced by countless variables beyond individual control
- Market dynamics appear increasingly complex and interconnected with broader cultural evolution
- Professional identity builds on capacity for learning rather than accumulated knowledge
- Growth means developing better questions about marketing challenges

This shift from certainty to curiosity, from answers to questions, from control to collaboration represents not a loss of expertise but its deepest expression. Master marketers know more than beginners precisely because they understand how much they don't know.

Marketing as Spiritual Practice

At the highest levels of development, marketing practice becomes indistinguishable from spiritual practice—not in any religious sense, but in the sense of work that consistently develops consciousness, serves authentic human needs, and contributes to both personal and collective evolution.

Characteristics of Marketing as Spiritual Practice

Present-Moment Awareness: Complete attention to current campaign requirements rather than being distracted by past successes or future anxieties about performance and results.

Ego Transcendence: Motivation centered on serving audience needs rather than enhancing personal reputation, status, or recognition within professional communities.

Continuous Learning: Genuine curiosity about improving effectiveness and authenticity rather than defending existing approaches or maintaining comfortable competence levels.

Interconnected Thinking: Recognition that marketing success depends on serving entire ecosystems rather than just immediate business objectives or short-term performance metrics.

Authentic Expression: Communication that emerges from genuine personal values and understanding rather than performed roles or adopted personas designed for strategic advantage.

Service Orientation: Primary focus on creating genuine value for others rather than extracting value from others through sophisticated persuasion or psychological manipulation.

This spiritual dimension doesn't diminish professional ambition or commercial effectiveness—it provides a foundation that enables greater risk-taking, more authentic innovation, and more sustainable success because the fundamental motivation remains constant even as external circumstances change.

The Daily Practice of Marketing Consciousness

Developing mastery-level marketing consciousness requires daily practices that go beyond technique development to encompass what we might call "consciousness cultivation"—systematic development of the internal qualities that enable consistent excellence.

Morning Foundation Practices

Intention Setting: Begin each day by clarifying your commitment to serving your audience's authentic needs rather than just achieving performance targets or professional advancement.

Presence Cultivation: Spend 10-15 minutes in meditation, contemplation, or mindful awareness practice to establish present-moment consciousness and reduce anxiety about outcomes.

Gratitude Recognition: Acknowledge specific aspects of your work, audience, and professional opportunities that you genuinely appreciate, creating a positive emotional foundation for creative and strategic thinking.

Learning Commitment: Identify one specific aspect of marketing psychology, audience understanding, or professional skill that you want to explore or develop during the day.

Working Practices

Single-Task Focus: Regularly practice sustained attention on individual marketing tasks without multitasking or digital distractions, building capacity for deep work and accessing the flow state.

Authenticity Checking: Before finalizing any marketing communication, pause to assess whether it feels genuine to your actual values and understanding rather than just strategically optimal.

Audience Empathy: Regularly imagine specific individuals from your target audience and consider how they might experience your marketing from their perspective rather than yours.

Curiosity Cultivation: Approach marketing challenges with genuine interest in discovering optimal solutions rather than immediately applying familiar approaches or defending existing strategies.

Evening Integration Practices

Reflection and Learning: Spend 5-10 minutes reviewing what you learned about marketing, human psychology, or your own creative process during the day.

Gratitude Expression: Acknowledge specific ways your work served others during the day, reinforcing service orientation rather than just personal achievement focus.

Tomorrow's Intention: Set a clear intention to approach the next day's marketing challenges with consciousness rather than just competence.

Release and Rest: Consciously release attachment to the day's outcomes and challenges, creating mental space for unconscious processing and restoration.

The Integration of Professional and Personal Development

Perhaps the most important insight about marketing mastery is that professional development and personal development are not separate processes; they are different aspects of the same consciousness evolution, serving both authentic self-expression and effective service to others.

Professional-Personal Integration Elements

Values Alignment: Ensuring that your marketing approaches reflect and express your genuine personal values rather than requiring you to compartmentalize different aspects of yourself.

Skill Development as Character Development: Recognizing that developing marketing capabilities also develops patience, creativity, empathy, resilience, and other qualities that enhance all aspects of life.

Work Relationships as Personal Growth: Approaching professional collaboration as opportunities for mutual learning and authentic connection rather than just transactional networking.

Success Redefinition: Measuring professional achievement by contribution to others' wellbeing and your own consciousness development rather than just external recognition or financial accumulation.

Challenge Transformation: Viewing professional difficulties as opportunities for developing greater wisdom, resilience, and service capacity rather than just obstacles to overcome.

Legacy Consideration: Making career decisions based on what kind of contribution you want to make to your field and culture rather than just immediate personal advantage.

This integration creates what we might call "conscious professionalism"—career development that serves both worldly success and spiritual growth through the same activities.

Actionable Exercises for Ongoing Development

Sustained marketing mastery requires specific practices that can be implemented immediately and developed consistently over time. These exercises address both technical skill development and consciousness cultivation.

Weekly Marketing Consciousness Exercises

The Audience Empathy Interview: Once per week, have a genuine conversation with someone from your target audience about their challenges, aspirations, and experiences—not to gather marketing intelligence, but to develop an authentic understanding and connection.

The Authenticity Audit: Review your recent marketing work and honestly assess which elements feel genuine to your values and understanding versus which feel performed or strategically calculated. Use this awareness to guide future authenticity development.

The Beginner's Mind Exercise: Choose one aspect of marketing that you consider yourself competent in and approach it as if you were learning it for the first time. What new insights emerge when you release expert assumptions?

The Service Impact Review: Examine specific ways your marketing work has genuinely helped people solve problems, achieve goals, or improve their lives. Use this recognition to reinforce service motivation.

Monthly Development Practices

The Learning Integration Session: Spend 2-3 hours each month reviewing what you've learned about marketing psychology, audience understanding, and professional development. How can these insights improve your future work?

The Values-Practice Alignment Check: Assess whether your current marketing approaches align with your personal values and long-term vision for your professional contribution. What adjustments might enhance this alignment?

The Feedback Integration Process: Gather and thoughtfully consider feedback from colleagues, customers, and other stakeholders about your marketing effectiveness and authenticity. How can this input inform your development?

The Consciousness Expansion Project: Choose one new area of study related to psychology, neuroscience, culture, or consciousness development that might enhance your marketing effectiveness and spend time exploring it systematically.

Quarterly Mastery Reviews

The Professional Purpose Reflection: Every three months, reflect deeply on why your marketing work matters to you personally and how it contributes to something larger than immediate business objectives.

The Mastery Goal Setting: Identify specific aspects of marketing consciousness you want to develop over the next quarter—not just technical skills but internal qualities like presence, authenticity, empathy, or resilience.

The Legacy Visioning Exercise: Imagine how you want to be remembered by colleagues, customers, and your industry. What qualities and contributions do you want to be known for? How does this vision guide current decisions?

The Integration Planning Process: Develop specific plans for how you will integrate insights from marketing psychology, consciousness development, and professional experience into your ongoing practice.

The Mentorship Dimension: Teaching as Learning

One of the most important aspects of lifelong marketing practice is the eventual transition from primarily learning from others to also teaching others—not because you have completed your own development, but because teaching deepens learning in ways that pure study cannot achieve.

The Learning-Teaching Cycle

Teaching Clarifies Understanding: Explaining marketing principles to others reveals gaps in your own understanding and forces deeper integration of psychological insights with practical experience.

Questions Stimulate Growth: Students and mentees ask questions that challenge your assumptions and push you to explore aspects of marketing you might not have considered independently.

Fresh Perspectives: Working with less experienced marketers provides exposure to new ways of thinking about familiar challenges and prevents ossification of your approaches.

Service Multiplication: Teaching enables your insights and development to serve more people than your individual marketing work alone could reach.

Humility Maintenance: Regular interaction with beginners reminds you of how much you once didn't know and how much you still don't know.

Formal and Informal Teaching Opportunities

- Mentoring junior colleagues or marketing professionals
- Writing articles, blog posts, or books about marketing insights
- Speaking at industry conferences or educational events
- Creating educational content or courses about marketing psychology
- Participating in professional communities and discussion forums
- Leading workshops or training sessions within your organization

The Evolution of Success Metrics

As marketing practice matures into lifelong development, the ways you measure success evolve beyond traditional performance indicators toward more integrated measures that encompass both commercial effectiveness and conscious contribution.

Traditional Success Metrics

- Campaign performance data and business results
- Professional recognition and industry awards
- Career advancement and financial compensation
- Market share growth and competitive positioning
- Client satisfaction and retention rates

Conscious Success Metrics

- Authentic service to audience genuine needs
- Personal consciousness development through professional practice
- Positive cultural contribution through marketing work
- Integration of personal values with professional activity
- Long-term relationship building with all stakeholders
- Knowledge sharing and mentorship contribution
- Sustainable practices that serve future generations

This evolution doesn't mean abandoning traditional metrics—it means placing them within a larger context that encompasses the full impact of your professional contribution.

The Technology Integration Challenge

As artificial intelligence and other technologies increasingly automate various aspects of marketing work, the challenge for conscious practitioners becomes integrating these tools in ways that enhance rather than replace human consciousness and authentic connection.

Conscious Technology Integration Principles

Human-AI Collaboration: Using artificial intelligence to handle analytical and optimization tasks while focusing human consciousness on creativity, empathy, and authentic communication.

Automation with Awareness: Automating routine marketing tasks while maintaining conscious involvement in strategic thinking and authentic audience service.

Data-Wisdom Synthesis: Combining technological data gathering with human wisdom about psychology, culture, and meaning that machines cannot replicate.

Efficiency-Authenticity Balance: Leveraging technology for efficiency while preserving the time and mental space necessary for genuine reflection, creativity, and conscious decision-making.

Scale-Intimacy Integration: Using technology to reach larger audiences while maintaining the authentic connection and personal care that characterizes conscious marketing.

The goal isn't to resist technological development but to integrate it consciously in ways that amplify rather than diminish the uniquely human capabilities that create genuine value.

The Legacy Perspective: Marketing as Cultural Contribution

At the highest level of development, marketing practice becomes a form of cultural stewardship—work that contributes not just to immediate business objectives but to the evolution of how marketing is practiced and how commercial activity serves human flourishing.

Cultural Legacy Elements

Elevating Industry Standards: Demonstrating that marketing can be both effective and ethical, both profitable and consciousness-developing, both strategic and authentic.

Mentoring Future Practitioners: Developing other marketers who will carry forward conscious approaches to commercial communication and business development.

Creating Positive Examples: Building brands and campaigns that demonstrate how conscious marketing serves both business success and genuine human needs.

Advancing Collective Understanding: Contributing to a broader understanding of how psychology, consciousness, and commerce can be integrated for mutual benefit.

Cultural Consciousness Evolution: Participating in the gradual transformation of business culture toward greater authenticity, service orientation, and consciousness development.

This legacy perspective provides long-term motivation, sustaining practice through inevitable challenges and changes, while ensuring that professional development serves something larger than individual advancement.

The Final Integration: Marketing as Life Practice

The ultimate goal of the inner game of marketing isn't just professional mastery but life mastery—the integration of marketing consciousness with overall human development in ways that serve both worldly effectiveness and spiritual growth.

Life Practice Integration

- Marketing consciousness enhances all communication and relationship skills
- Business challenges become opportunities for developing patience, creativity, and resilience
- Professional service extends into all life activities and relationships
- Authentic self-expression through marketing supports authentic self-expression in all contexts
- Success becomes measured by contribution to others' wellbeing rather than just personal achievement
- Work becomes a form of meditation and consciousness development

When marketing practice achieves this level of integration, the boundaries between profession and purpose, work and worship, success and service begin to dissolve. The practice becomes both means and end—a way of developing consciousness that naturally expresses itself through effective marketing that genuinely serves human flourishing.

The Continuous Beginning

Perhaps the most important insight about marketing as a lifelong practice is that mastery represents not an end point but a continuous beginning—each campaign, each challenge, each success, and each failure becomes a fresh opportunity to deepen understanding, enhance authenticity, and improve service to others.

The inner game of marketing never ends because human consciousness continues evolving, cultural dynamics keep changing, and new opportunities for authentic service constantly emerge. The goal isn't to achieve perfect marketing capability but to develop the kind of conscious competence that enables continuous learning and growing while consistently creating valuable work.

This perspective transforms marketing from a career you pursue into a practice you develop, from work you do into consciousness you cultivate, from success you achieve into service you provide. When marketing is approached as lifelong practice, it becomes both personally fulfilling and professionally effective while contributing to the kind of cultural evolution that serves everyone it touches.

The journey of the inner game of marketing has no final destination—only the continuous deepening of consciousness, authenticity, and service that makes each day's work both an expression of who you are and a contribution to who you are becoming. This is both the challenge and the gift of marketing mastery: it demands everything you have to give while giving you everything you need to grow.

Welcome to the practice. The work begins now, continues forever, and serves everyone it touches when approached with the consciousness we have explored throughout this journey together.

Bibliography

Core Foundational Works

1. Gallwey, W. Timothy. The Inner Game of Tennis: The Classic Guide to the Mental Side of Peak Performance. Rev. ed. New York: Random House, 1997.
   The seminal work that originated the inner game approach demonstrated how psychological mastery enables peak performance in any complex skill domain.
2. Kahneman, Daniel. Thinking, Fast and Slow. New York: Farrar, Straus and Giroux, 2011. Essential foundation for understanding System 1 and System 2 thinking that underlies both marketer decision-making and consumer behavior.
3. Csikszentmihalyi, Mihaly. Flow: The Psychology of Optimal Experience. New York: Harper & Row, 1990. Fundamental research on flow states that provides the neurological foundation for peak marketing performance and authentic audience connection.

Case Resources

1. Belk, Russell W. "Extended Self in Consumer Behavior." Journal of Consumer Research 15, no. 2 (September 1988): 139–168.
2. Goldman, Robert, and Stephen Papson. Nike Culture: The Sign of the Swoosh. Thousand Oaks, CA: Sage Publications, 1998.
3. Holt, Douglas B. How Brands Become Icons: The Principles of Cultural Branding. Boston: Harvard Business School Press, 2004.
4. Isaacson, Walter. Steve Jobs. New York: Simon & Schuster, 2011.
5. Katz, Donald. Just Do It: The Nike Spirit in the Corporate World. New York: Random House, 1994.

6. Zak, Paul J. "Why Inspiring Stories Make Us React: The Neuroscience of Narrative." Cerebrum (2015).
7. Zak, Paul J. "The Neurobiology of Trust." Scientific American, January 2017.
8. Barraza, Jorge A., and Paul J. Zak. "Empathy toward Strangers Triggers Oxytocin Release and Subsequent Generosity." Annals of the New York Academy of Sciences 1167 (2009): 182–189.

Theoretical Foundations

1. Ambady, Nalini, and Robert Rosenthal. "Thin Slices of Expressive Behavior as Predictors of Interpersonal Consequences." Psychological Bulletin 111, no. 2 (1992): 256–274.
2. Ariely, Dan. Predictably Irrational: The Hidden Forces That Shape Our Decisions. New York: HarperCollins, 2008.
3. Berridge, Kent C., and Terry E. Robinson. "What Is the Role of Dopamine in Reward? Hedonic Impact, Reward Learning, or Incentive Salience?" Brain Research Reviews 28, no. 3 (1998): 309–369.
4. Csikszentmihalyi, Mihaly. Flow: The Psychology of Optimal Experience. New York: Harper & Row, 1990.
5. Csikszentmihalyi, Mihaly. Creativity: Flow and the Psychology of Discovery and Invention. New York: HarperCollins, 1996.
6. Dweck, Carol S. Mindset: The New Psychology of Success. New York: Random House, 2006.
7. Edmondson, Amy C. The Fearless Organization: Creating Psychological Safety in the Workplace for Learning, Innovation, and Growth. Hoboken, NJ: John Wiley & Sons, 2018.
8. Gallese, Vittorio. "The Roots of Empathy: The Shared Manifold Hypothesis and the Neural Basis of Intersubjectivity." Psychopathology 36, no. 4 (2003): 171–180.
9. Gallwey, W. Timothy. The Inner Game of Tennis. New York: Random House, 1974.
10. Gladwell, Malcolm. Blink: The Power of Thinking Without Thinking. New York: Little, Brown and Company, 2005.

11. Green, Melanie C., and Timothy C. Brock. "The Role of Transportation in the Persuasiveness of Public Narratives." Journal of Personality and Social Psychology 79, no. 5 (2000): 701–721.
12. Iacoboni, Marco. Mirroring People: The New Science of How We Connect with Others. New York: Farrar, Straus and Giroux, 2008.
13. Kahneman, Daniel. Thinking, Fast and Slow. New York: Farrar, Straus and Giroux, 2011.
14. Kounios, John, and Mark Beeman. The Eureka Factor: Aha Moments, Creative Insight, and the Brain. New York: Random House, 2015.
15. Loftus, Elizabeth F. Eyewitness Testimony. Cambridge, MA: Harvard University Press, 1996.
16. Rizzolatti, Giacomo, Corrado Sinigaglia. Mirrors in the Brain: How Our Minds Share Actions and Emotions. Oxford: Oxford University Press, 2008.
17. Sawyer, R. Keith. Group Genius: The Creative Power of Collaboration. New York: Basic Books, 2007.
18. Schacter, Daniel L. The Seven Sins of Memory: How the Mind Forgets and Remembers. Boston: Houghton Mifflin, 2001.
19. Schultz, Wolfram. "Dopamine Reward Prediction Error Coding." Journal of Neurophysiology 80, no. 1 (1998): 1–27.
20. Schultz, Wolfram. "Multiple Dopamine Functions at Different Time Courses." Annual Review of Neuroscience 30 (2007): 259–288.
21. Stanovich, Keith E., and Richard F. West. "Individual Differences in Reasoning: Implications for the Rationality Debate." Behavioral and Brain Sciences 23, no. 5 (2000): 645–726.
22. Tversky, Amos, and Daniel Kahneman. "Judgment under Uncertainty: Heuristics and Biases." Science 185, no. 4157 (September 1974): 1124–1131.
23. Zaltman, Gerald. How Customers Think: Essential Insights into the Mind of the Market. Boston: Harvard Business School Press, 2003.

Case Resources

1. Belk, Russell W. "Extended Self in Consumer Behavior." Journal of Consumer Research 15, no. 2 (September 1988): 139–168.

2. Goldman, Robert, and Stephen Papson. Nike Culture: The Sign of the Swoosh. Thousand Oaks, CA: Sage Publications, 1998.
3. Holt, Douglas B. How Brands Become Icons: The Principles of Cultural Branding. Boston: Harvard Business School Press, 2004.
4. Isaacson, Walter. Steve Jobs. New York: Simon & Schuster, 2011.
5. Katz, Donald. Just Do It: The Nike Spirit in the Corporate World. New York: Random House, 1994.
6. Zak, Paul J. "Why Inspiring Stories Make Us React: The Neuroscience of Narrative." Cerebrum (2015).
7. Zak, Paul J. "The Neurobiology of Trust." Scientific American, January 2017.
8. Barraza, Jorge A., and Paul J. Zak. "Empathy toward Strangers Triggers Oxytocin Release and Subsequent Generosity." Annals of the New York Academy of Sciences 1167 (2009): 182–189.

Note

Case resources document publicly available brand histories and applied empirical studies. Theoretical foundations provide the scientific and conceptual basis for the book's arguments.

The Inner Game of Marketing

This glossary provides clear definitions of the key concepts, psychological principles, and specialized terminology used throughout *The Inner Game of Marketing*. These terms represent the integration of insights from psychology, neuroscience, consciousness studies, and marketing practice that form the foundation of the inner game approach.

A

Anchoring Bias

The cognitive tendency for initial information to disproportionately influence subsequent judgments. In marketing contexts, the first price, quality impression, or brand encounter establishes an unconscious reference point that shapes all future evaluations. Understanding anchoring enables marketers to deliberately establish favorable reference points rather than leaving crucial first impressions to chance.

Attention Architecture

The systematic design of marketing campaigns that naturally align with neurological attention patterns rather than fighting against them. This includes understanding pre-attention filtering, attention capture dynamics, sustained engagement requirements, memory encoding triggers, and action motivation systems.

Authentic Performance

The integration of genuine values and strategic effectiveness where authenticity enhances rather than constrains performance. Distinguished from "performing authenticity," which simulates genuine expression for strategic purposes. Authentic performance emerges when skilled execution serves genuine understanding and sincere desire to create value.

Availability Bias

The tendency to judge probability and importance based on how easily examples come to mind. For brands, this creates both opportunities (making positive experiences more mentally accessible) and vulnerabilities (negative recent experiences overshadowing positive history). Effective marketing increases the cognitive availability of positive brand associations.

B

Behavioral Consistency Monitoring

The brain's unconscious process of tracking whether observed behavior aligns with stated values over time. This neurological authenticity detection system builds trust when words and actions are congruent and triggers skepticism when they contradict each other. Essential for building genuine brand credibility.

Brand Lust

A neurochemical state where desire for a product transcends rational evaluation of need or value, created through sophisticated activation of dopamine reward prediction systems. Distinguished from temporary want or logical preference by its intensity and resistance to rational analysis.

C

Category Design

The strategic approach of creating new market categories rather than competing within existing ones. Category design transforms zero-sum competition for market share into positive-sum category growth where success comes from expanding possibilities rather than capturing existing demand.

Category King

A company that doesn't just lead a market category but defines what the category itself means. Category kings achieve this position by systematically redefining customer expectations, establishing new evaluation criteria, and building ecosystem infrastructure that reinforces their definitional authority.

Cognitive Flexibility

The mental agility to consider multiple explanations for unexpected results, shift perspectives when new information emerges, and adapt frameworks when existing approaches prove inadequate. Essential for resilient learning and effective adaptation to changing market conditions.

Confirmation Bias

The tendency to preferentially notice and remember information that confirms existing beliefs while minimizing attention to contradictory evidence. In marketing contexts, this creates both loyalty lock-in for satisfied customers and resistance to change among dissatisfied ones.

Conscious Competence

The integration of sophisticated knowledge with intuitive execution where psychological understanding informs work without overwhelming the creative process. At this level, principles become second nature, enabling both analytical rigor and authentic expression.

Conscious Practice

Deliberately applying psychological insights in real marketing contexts while paying attention to both internal experience and external results. Distinguished from unconscious practice (doing without awareness) and purely analytical study (understanding without application).

Conviction Transmission

The neurological process by which genuine confidence about value propositions unconsciously influences audience receptiveness through mirror neuron activation and emotional contagion. Authentic conviction reduces resistance and facilitates decision-making more effectively than persuasion techniques.

Creative Courage

The ability to act effectively in the presence of uncertainty, accepting that you cannot know with complete certainty how campaigns will perform while remaining committed to authentic value creation. Distinguished from fearlessness by its integration of both vulnerability and determination.

D

Default Mode Network

Brain regions active during rest that are involved in self-referential thinking, moral reasoning, and imagining future scenarios. In marketing contexts, content that activates this network through personal relevance or future simulation creates stronger engagement and memory formation.

Dopamine Prediction Error

The neurochemical mechanism where dopamine release peaks during anticipation of reward rather than receipt of reward. Understanding this system enables marketers to create anticipation loops that generate more engagement than the actual product experience itself.

E

Embodied Cognition

The neurological phenomenon where the brain processes narratives not as abstract information but as vicarious experience, activating the same neural networks involved in actually living through similar events. This explains why authentic stories create more influence than logical arguments.

Experimental Mindset

The psychological orientation that treats campaign results as information about market dynamics rather than verdicts about personal competence. This mindset enables faster learning and adaptation by reducing defensive responses to unexpected outcomes.

F

Flow State

A neurological condition characterized by complete absorption in activity, effortless concentration, and optimal performance. In marketing contexts, flow states enable the integration of analytical thinking with creative insight, producing work that feels both sophisticated and authentic.

Future Simulation

The brain's capacity to imagine potential future scenarios, heavily involved in decision-making and motivation. Effective marketing activates future simulation by helping customers envision improved possibilities that include the marketed offering.

G

Grounded Conviction

Authentic confidence that remains connected to external reality and responsive to genuine feedback. Distinguished from overconfidence or delusion by its integration of inner certainty with ongoing learning and adaptation.

H

Halo Effect

The tendency for impressions in one area to influence opinions in unrelated areas. Strong brands leverage halo effects where positive associations in one dimension (innovation, quality, trustworthiness) automatically transfer to other dimensions in customer perception.

I

Incentive Salience

The psychological state where obtaining something becomes compellingly important regardless of its objective utility. Created through sophisticated activation of dopamine pathways, incentive salience explains why people engage in behaviors that exceed rational cost-benefit analysis.

Inner Critic

The internal voice of doubt, criticism, and catastrophic prediction that often interferes with authentic creative expression. Distinguished from legitimate analytical concerns by its generalized negativity and lack of specific, actionable feedback.

Inner Game

The internal psychological dynamics that determine external performance quality. Originally developed by Tim Gallwey for tennis, the inner game approach focuses on removing internal interference rather than adding external techniques.

L

Limbic System

The brain region responsible for emotion, memory formation, and social bonding. Marketing that effectively engages the limbic system through authentic emotional connection often proves more influential than purely rational appeals to the neocortex.

M

Marketing Consciousness

An integrated way of being and working where sophisticated psychological understanding naturally informs marketing practice without constraining authentic expression. This represents the synthesis of analytical competence with intuitive wisdom in service of genuine value creation.

Mirror Neurons

Specialized brain cells that fire both when performing an action and when observing someone else perform the same action. These neurons create automatic neurological empathy and explain why authentic emotional expressions in marketing generate corresponding responses in audiences.

N

Neural Mirroring

The unconscious synchronization of brain states between observer and observed. In marketing contexts, audiences' mirror neurons respond to the authentic emotional and psychological states of people in marketing content, making genuine expression more influential than performed emotion.

Neocortex

The brain region responsible for rational analysis, language processing, and future planning. While important for processing logical information, the neocortex typically provides post-decision justification for choices made by deeper brain systems.

Novelty Detection

The brain's specialized systems for identifying information that's different from established patterns. Genuine novelty receives priority processing and enhanced memory formation, making authentic innovation more effective than incremental improvement for capturing attention.

O

Oxytocin

Often called the "trust hormone," this neurochemical is released during positive social interactions and experiences of empathy. Stories that follow specific narrative patterns can trigger oxytocin release, creating neurochemical states associated with trust and social bonding.

P

Peak-End Rule

The psychological principle that people remember experiences primarily based on the peak (most intense moment) and the end (final moment), with duration and average quality having surprisingly little impact on memory and evaluation.

Presence

Complete attention to current creative and strategic demands rather than being distracted by past campaigns or future anxieties. Presence enables access to both analytical thinking and intuitive insight while maintaining awareness of audience needs and market realities.

Psychological Aikido

The approach of working with rather than against existing forces in customer consciousness, redirecting psychological patterns toward mutual benefit rather than trying to overcome them through superior force or manipulation.

R

Reptilian Brain

The brain stem and cerebellum governing survival instincts and automatic responses. This ancient system responds to marketing that addresses fundamental needs like safety, status, and resource acquisition, often triggering immediate approach or avoidance responses.

Resonance Model

The approach of identifying and amplifying preferences that already exist but may not be fully conscious, rather than trying to change customer preferences through persuasion. Resonance eliminates resistance by aligning with existing psychological realities.

S

Self 1

In Gallwey's framework, the conscious, analytical, controlling voice that wants to get everything right and avoid mistakes. While valuable for strategic planning, Self 1 can interfere with natural competence when it becomes overly dominant during execution.

Self 2

The unconscious, intuitive, naturally competent voice that knows how to communicate authentically and recognizes what feels genuine versus forced. Self 2 operates through pattern recognition and embodied wisdom rather than analytical frameworks.

Serial Position Effect

The tendency to remember information from the beginning and end of sequences better than information from the middle. This affects how marketing messages should be structured to ensure important content receives adequate attention and encoding.

Social Proof

The psychological tendency to look to others' behavior for guidance about appropriate action, especially in uncertain situations. Effective marketing provides authentic social proof rather than manufactured testimonials or false consensus indicators.

Systemic Listening

Attention to the complex web of relationships, values, and consequences that surround business decisions, going beyond immediate customer feedback to include cultural, environmental, and long-term stakeholder considerations.

System 1 Thinking

Fast, automatic, and intuitive mental processing that operates below conscious awareness, generating immediate impressions and creative insights. Essential for authentic communication and cultural attunement in marketing.

System 2 Thinking

Slow, deliberate, and analytical mental processing responsible for logical reasoning and conscious evaluation. Important for strategic planning and optimization but can interfere with authenticity if overly dominant during creative execution.

T

Thin-Slice Judgments

Rapid, automatic assessments based on minimal information that are often more accurate than extended deliberate analysis. Experienced marketers develop sophisticated thin-slice capabilities for evaluating campaign potential and audience response.

Transient Hypofrontality

The temporary downregulation of the prefrontal cortex during flow states, creating freedom from self-criticism and analytical overthinking that often interferes with peak creative performance.

Transportation

The psychological experience of being absorbed into a narrative world, where the boundary between self and story character becomes blurred. Effective marketing storytelling creates transportation that enables audiences to experience rather than just observe value propositions.

U

Unconscious Competence

The ability to perform complex tasks effectively without conscious effort or attention. In marketing, this represents the integration of psychological principles with practical skills to the point where sophisticated understanding enhances rather than constrains natural expression.

V

Variable Ratio Reinforcement

Reward schedules where timing or magnitude varies unpredictably, creating higher levels of engagement than fixed, predictable patterns. Social media platforms and effective email marketing often employ variable ratio schedules to maintain audience attention.

Verdict Mindset

The psychological orientation that treats campaign results as judgments about personal competence rather than information about market dynamics. This mindset creates defensive responses that interfere with learning and adaptation.

W

Working Memory

The cognitive system that holds immediate conscious awareness, with extremely limited capacity and brief duration. Understanding working memory constraints is crucial for creating marketing messages that can be effectively processed and retained.

About the Author

Subba Rao Chaganti is a pioneering voice at the intersection of pharmaceutical marketing, behavioral science, and emerging technologies. With over three decades of industry experience and a prolific portfolio of 30+ groundbreaking books on pharmaceutical strategy, Chaganti is widely regarded as a thought leader who redefines how pharma educates, engages, and empowers.

He began his journey as a marketing educator and practitioner, driven by a singular mission: to bridge the gap between science and storytelling in pharma. Today, his work spans disciplines—from sales force effectiveness and key account management to digital therapeutics, wearable tech, internal branding, and AI-powered brand strategy.

Beyond the books, Chaganti is a mentor to brand managers, a respected voice on LinkedIn and Substack, and an unwavering advocate for ethical, patient-centered innovation in life sciences marketing. His ability to translate complexity into actionable strategy makes his work not just readable—but indispensable.

He lives in Farmington, Connecticut, USA, and can be reached at: subbarao.chaganti@gmail.com.

Here is a list of his publications:

1. Pharmaceutical Marketing in India: Concepts, Cases, Strategy
2. Game Plans for Post-GATT Era: Action Agenda of the Indian Pharmaceutical Industry
3. Compete or Forfeit: Strategies for Sustainable Competitive Advantage in the Pharma Product Patents Era
4. Pharmaceutical Marketing in India for Today and Tomorrow - 25th Anniversary Edition
5. Bullseyes and Blunders: Lessons from 100 Cases in Pharma Marketing
6. Digital Pharma Marketing Playbook: Winning With the New Rules of Engagement

7. Cracking the Generics Code: Your Single-Source Success Manual for Winning in Multi-Source Product Markets
8. Reimagine Pharma Marketing: Make It Future-Proof!
9. Brand Positioning in Pharma
10. Transactional to Transformational Marketing in Pharma: The Science of Why and The Art of How
11. A to Z of Pharmaceutical Marketing: World's First and Only Encyclopedia in Two Volumes
12. The Synergy of Minds: Human+AI Orchestrating the Pharma Marketing Revolution
13. Design Thinking for Pharma
14. The Pharma Product Manager: Navigating the Digital Frontier
15. Sentiment Analysis for Pharma Marketers
16. Whispering to AI: Prompt Engineering for Pharma Brand Managers
17. Storytelling in Pharma Marketing
18. Beyond the Molecule: The Art and Science of Metaphors That Matter
19. The Voices Within: Your Body Speaks, When your organs tell their own stories
20. Pharma Archetypes: The Science of Meaningful Healthcare Marketing
21. Navigating the AI Revolution: Human Futures
22. Breaking Through: A Business Novel (based on the theory of constraints)
23. The Wearable Edge: Redefining Pharma Marketing in a Connected and Data-Driven World
24. Code to Cure: Digital Therapeutics and the Future of Pharma
25. Level Up: Gamification in Pharma Marketing

www.ingramcontent.com/pod-product-compliance
Ingram Content Group UK Ltd.
Pitfield, Milton Keynes, MK11 3LW, UK
UKHW020125290926
15471UKWH00003B/300

9 789347 311178